I0482807

Small to **Medium Size Business TECHNOLOGY**

A Step-by-Step **Guide**

Choosing the RIGHT Hardware and Software for YOUR Business

by Vinrose NALUYANGE

ACKNOWLEDGMENT

To every person who has contributed to the success of this book. Most significantly, my parents John and Justine Seruyange for all the support.

Dr. Nathan Muyinda, Juko Sara, and Loy Kwagala for their time and expert advice, and the following people for understanding my long nights at the computer: Veron Nabulime, Derek Muyanja, Noeline Nanyonga, Rogers Seruyange, and Resty Namuyanja.

Finally, thank you to my coach Mr. Geoffrey Semaganda (ActionWealthPublishing.com), who taught me the ropes. I am truly grateful for your support and your many hours of working on this book. Thank you.

TABLE OF CONTENTS

INTRODUCTION

Running a business in today's climate of competitiveness and fragile economics comes with many challenges. There are certain strategies that micro enterprises, small businesses and medium- sized organisations can utilise in order to make the running of their business easier and more profitable. Choosing the right kind of technology is one of them.

Do you opt for Windows or do you choose Apple? Not so many years ago, this would have been the fundamental question that small- to medium-size enterprises (SMEs) would have had to ask themselves. Their computer hardware and software options would have been very much defined by this simple question. Today however, it is a completely different story and thanks to the vast array of technology available, the Windows versus Apple dilemma is not so much of a pertinent question.

For an SME to realistically compete in today's increasingly competitive world, the type of technology they use is paramount to their success. With the right technology, SMEs can improve customer experiences and interactions; they can increase mobility options and operational efficiencies.

While SME owners realise the importance of executing the right kind of technology, many feel choosing which hardware and software to employ in their business strategy is like trying to find a needle in a haystack.

If you are about to embark on launching your business, or are an established SME who would like to improve your enterprise's technological infrastructure, and are unsure about where to get started with your business's technology requirements, then take a look at the following step-by-step guide on small- to medium-size business technology.

This step-by-step guide will explore the most crucial elements of developing a successful technological system that includes the right mix of hardware and software in order to make your SME more profitable, less inclined for failure and generally better equipped for more expansion and success.

The various chapters will look at companies' goals and why SMEs need technology. It will consider SME's technological concerns and trade-offs, budgets and where to get advice on such issues.

The guide will explore different infrastructure systems and services and readers will be more aware of concepts such as automated systems, access management systems, network management systems and digital surveillance systems.

This comprehensive guide to infrastructure systems and services also includes advice on network architecture and design, unified communication and VoIP.

Being proficient at recovering quickly from any IT disasters your business may experience, would be an expedient quality of all SMEs that rely on technology. This eBook aims to inform its readers of disaster recovery and business continuity.

Being firmly entrenched in the digital era, the internet is an invaluable tool for most businesses, large or small. It is therefore all but imperative that SMEs have sound knowledge of the 'information highway' and all the profits and pitfalls the internet can generate.

So sit back, relax and take a look at the following step-by-step guide on small- to medium-sized business technology and how to get started on choosing the right hardware and software for your business. You never know, reading this eBook could mean the difference between success and failure.

1

COMPANY AND TECHNOLOGY

You may be surprised to learn that, when it comes to technology, many businesses have very similar needs. Depending on which industry you are embarking, there will be some specific technologies that you will require and that another industry would have no requirements for.

The surmise that smaller businesses rely on their technology more than larger companies is a controversial statement. There is, however, an element of truth attached to this contentious declaration. For example, if a small business suddenly found itself faced with an IT problem, it would mean that its employees would not be able to work efficiently. Given the fact that this handful of employees are likely to make up quite a large percentage of the company's whole workforce, there would be a big chance that the SME would be more adversely affected by the IT breakdown than a larger company.

It is therefore imperative that SMEs align a technology strategy in their business plan. Carrying out this prudent move would mean that, if an IT problem did occur, the business would be less prone to being negatively affected.

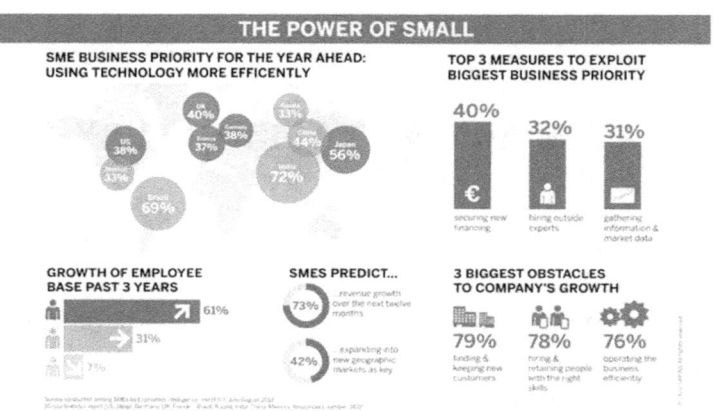

As you read through this book it should come as no surprise that technology is intrinsically linked to success for most small businesses. Around the world, technology is a priority because of its power to drive a business forward and allow micro, small and medium sized business to hit above their weight. (Source: http://en.sap.info/eiu-sme-opportunities-emerging-markets/81771/2)

Every business IT plan should include the goals it wants its hardware and software to achieve, so that it is exceptionally clear how a company focus on technology will move the organisation forward towards its stated aims and objectives.

Whether it is a high speed internet connection that enables employees to carry out internet research quickly and efficiently, or utilising a network of spreadsheets in order to track and monitor orders, every business should execute a solid IT plan.

This will then help the company determine what type of technology it does and doesn't need. Once the bigger pictures of the technological necessities of a company have been determined, SMEs can then seek advice on which specific hardware and software to incorporate into their business.

The most pressing challenges facing SMEs today are competition and rising costs. These two leading company concerns are quickly followed by worries about business continuity, risk and disaster recovery. Cost is therefore a prevailing influence in an SME's choice of technology. For most start-ups and even established SMEs wanting to update their computer systems, choosing hardware and software that is within their budget is vital.

In this chapter we will look at the different technological goals companies have: why SMEs need to implement an IT system; the leading concerns many companies have when it comes to technology, and the trade-offs. Trade-offs are a big part of making any kind of new technology and this step-by-step guide will explore some of the most common technological trade-offs facing many contemporary companies.

The chapter will also explore when an SME might need technological advice; how such advice may prove vital, and where business owners can turn to for technological advice.

Finally, similar to all walks of life, the type of hardware and software a business can implement is significantly determined by the SMEs budget. We will take a look at how a business's budget can influence the type of technology a business can put into operation.

COMING UP:

▼ The Big Picture (Company Goals)

▼ Why Technology

▼ Technology in SME:
the concerns and trade-offs

▼ Get advice

▼ Company Budgets

2

THE BIG PICTURE

One of the many jobs a business owner is faced with is constantly planning for the future. In order to witness company growth, existing products and services evolve, new services are implemented, additional employees are taken on and other areas of the business expanded.

Tenacious business owners are confident about trading conditions and are looking to expand in 2013 and beyond. In fact, since the offset of 2013, it has been an optimistic year as far as entrepreneurs and business owners are concerned.

It is within every SME's interest, as it is with larger corporations, to upscale and grow. This rather sweeping statement can be backed up with research made by Aviva's bi-annual SME Pulse review. The report, released in January this year, revealed that as many as 65% of the participating SMEs expected strong sale averages during the first half of 2013. This contrasted significantly with the 2012 report, which showed that just 32% of SMEs expected decent sale averages during the first half of that year.

This renewed sense of optimism within the world of SMEs, has translated into more ambitious business targets and new goals and objectives being planned by SME owners. The Aviva research revealed that more than one third of the SMEs, which participated in the study, are looking to expand their business as a means of making revenue increases.

Besides expanding on the amount of products it sells, services it offers and increasing the amount of staff a company has on its books, one of the most effectual ways a business can attain its goals of expansion is to improve its IT infrastructure and technological capabilities.

The savviest of entrepreneurs will establish both long-term and short-term goals. As Forbes advises, "create long-term goals (such as 'double revenue by the end of the second year of business') to provide milestones to help you visualise progress for the years to come."

These long-term goals should be accompanied by short-term goals – monthly, quarterly and yearly objectives – that will help an enterprise to gradually edge closer to achieving its longer-term goals.

In order to achieve these goals, the shrewdest of business owners implement a technology road map. With the right technology investments, a modern business, whether it is a small start-up, an established medium-sized business or an international corporation, will be better equipped to advance towards its goals. With the correct IT system and hardware and software in place, a business can be launched into a higher level of performance and achievement.

In order for a business to match its growth and technology goals, it should begin by looking at its overall business strategy. A company owner should ask themselves where they want their business to be in the next five, ten or 15 years time? They should also ask themselves, what role will technology play in achieving this growth?

Once an SME has determined the scope and structure of its business plan, it will then need to define the role that technology will play in each stage of the planned growth.

3

WHY TECHNOLOGY?

Technology can help businesses achieve these long-term and short-term goals. How, you might ask yourself? Well, if you think back several decades ago to how business was carried out, it was substantially different to today. There was no email, no internet, no mobile marketing, no smartphones or telecommuting from remote locations around the world.

Today, with the arrival and prolific rise of the digital era and technology we now know and love, communication is instantaneous. A vast amount of information is sent and received almost instantaneously through email. Instead of having to physically correspond with employees, clients and colleagues either face-to-face or on the telephone, correspondence can be achieved quickly and efficiently through the internet. Innovations in technology have meant that the productivity of a workforce is infinitely more efficient, which ultimately meant that companies, of all sizes, are better equipped in achieving their short-term and long-term goals and enable them to edge their way from a small start-up in the first year into a global empire the next.

According to a study released by CompTIA, the non-profit trade association for the IT industry, technology enables SMEs to become more mobile and competitive. Increasingly, small- and medium-sized businesses are using technology to improve their interactions with customers, their operational efficiencies and their options regarding mobility.

According to CompTIA's *Third Annual Small and Medium Business Technology Adoptions Trends* study, from 2011 – 2012, seven out of ten businesses surveyed expected to expand technology spending during the next twelve months.

"Technology is more accessible, more affordable and more available to SMBs than ever before," said Seth Robinson, CompTIA's director and technology analysis.

"SMBs may not have an abundance of capital to invest, so they have to make every dollar count. But the majority are willing to spend money on new technologies, especially solutions that give them capabilities on part with a larger enterprise. Technology plays an integral role in the life of a small business," Seth Robinson continues.

The rise of mobile technology is becoming increasingly prevalent in company growth. One only has to look at the way commuters on a train feverishly finger their smartphones. While some might be sending text messages to loved ones or playing games to drown out the boredom of the journey, many are searching for products and services as they commute to work.

Going mobile has been deemed as being "essential" for business survival. Given the fact that smartphone activity converts to action, both offline and online, and that approximately 55% of follow up action on a smartphone happens within one hour of users carrying out the search, the imperativeness of utilising mobile technology is understandable.

Along with this new focus on mobile technology, the practise of BOYD or bring your own device (sometimes called BYOT or bring your own technology) has emerged. Some studies suggest that as many as 75% of all workers in growing markets such as Brazil and Russia are already using their own devices at work to get ahead. Elsewhere, around 44% of employees use their own technology regularly to help them do their job (source: Ovum's multi-market Q4 2012 BYOD survey).

Whether you run a small hairdressing business or an increasingly expanding web design company, you will need computers to log information, track clients, record invoices, and so on. The exact specifications will depend on each individual business and its specific needs. Suffice it to say, SMEs serious about getting ahead need the best possible equipment for the job. As a basic rule of thumb, each computer within a business should have ample memory and a high quality screen so that employees are at minimal risk of eye strain. Having a quality, high-speed network of computers in place will ensure a business will be able to store, manage and back up valuable files and data.

4

TECHNOLOGY IN SMES: CONCERNS AND TRADE-OFFS

We have established that in order for a small- to medium-sized business to survive, thrive and expand, technology is paramount. Although with the growth and prolific advances in technology in recent years, a new set of problems and concerns arise for many SMEs. With IT giants, such as Google, announcing ambitious plans to tap small and medium enterprise segments for their solutions, a new debate has occurred over whether or not SMEs are actually prepared to adopt the emerging technology for their growth.

SMEs have their own concerns regarding their receptiveness to emerging technology. Research house, David Lewis Consultancy conducted a survey on the top technology concerns facing SMEs today. The survey targeted business owners, CEOs and MDs of businesses based in the UK, which ranged from between five employees to 500 staff. Almost 70% of the respondents said that cost was the leading factor which influenced their choice of technology.

A majority of the respondents acknowledged that technological innovation is a leading component in creating a successful business that is able to compete in the market. 80% of the respondents said that innovations within technology and new business solutions are altering the culture of the SME industry and are now vital to the growth and success of smaller businesses.

Despite the majority of the business owners and CEOs recognising and understanding the importance of technological advancement in order to nurture growth, more than half of the survey participators agreed that their existing infrastructure was not secure enough.

Whilst inferior existing IT infrastructures and a lack of financial resources to fund the implementing of a newer, more advanced technology system are the leading technology concerns facing SMEs today, a quarter of the respondents cited business continuity, risk and disaster recovery as being the third most pertinent challenge. A considerably lower percentage of the participants indicated that IT software and solutions were not considered a key challenge for SMEs.

In today's fragile economy, the costs of advancing hardware and software systems are naturally a major concern that hampers many SME's growth. The expense of the power crisis failing the industry, the costs of overheads involved in hosting a company's internet presence and the need to employ experienced and trained employees to manage websites, social media accounts and update such information regularly, are components of modern technology that many SMEs are finding it difficult to financially resource.

"They might have their own projections. But for the SMEs which are already struggling to manage their daily affairs, it is not going to be an easy task," said S.P.K. Reddy, president of the Federation of Small and Medium Enterprises.

Reddy recalled the closure of hundreds of small and micro units due to frequent power failures; these came at a heavy price to struggling SMEs. Reiterating that technology costs are a major concern facing SMEs today, ITsAP managing community member, Ramesh Loganathan, said that an upfront investment on IT systems was a major problem many SMEs faced today. Although the ITsAP managing community member suggested that with the utilisation of cloud technology, investments in procuring software and hardware are not so problematic.

"Now that the services are hosted on the cloud, it should not be a problem," said Ramesh Loganathan.

Implementing the cloud is certainly a cost effective solution for SMEs as they do not have to pay for licensed hardware or software. As Loganathan says:

"It is a pay for use model which the small enterprises should not find difficult to manage."

A recent study commissioned by Microsoft, which surveyed 107 SMEs in the UK, found that two thirds of the SMEs that have moved their software and hardware services to the cloud had made savings. However, this has created a new set of problems and concerns for many SMEs. Data security is the main concern that SMEs in the UK have with regard to adopting cloud services. 52% of the companies that participated in the Microsoft commissioned survey, and which do not currently use the cloud, said that data security concerns were "an inhibitor to adoption".

In addition to data concerns:

What are the main concerns of non-cloud computer users?

- 51% are concerned about reliability

- 45% of SMEs fear that they will lose control of their data

- 31% have concerns about regulatory compliance

According to the Microsoft survey, a third of the companies that do not use the cloud agreed that if industry standards were set and government regulation enforced, it would increase the likelihood of the companies adopting cloud technology.

While trade-offs are everywhere in life, perhaps the most obvious trade-offs occur in technology. Technological change is always accompanied with a trade-off, as no technology is without its downsides.

The trade-off versus advantages model is different with every kind of technology. As an extreme example, we could cite the pyramids, which were an incredible technological construction which the world still marvels today, but they came at a trade-off that surely wasn't worth it – slave labour.

The same could be said about those SMEs struggling to afford the time, expertise and money to employ a social media expert into their business. The SME owner knows that in order to be more competitive in his trade, he should adopt a solid social media strategy, but the trade-off would be the financial resources he would need to find to adopt such a strategy.

There is perhaps no better way to explain the technological trade-off model than in cloud services. As the Microsoft study revealed, SMEs that implement the cloud find themselves with a cost-effective hardware and software solution; but the lack of control over such data could be seen as a trade-off for this type of technology.

5

GET ADVICE

In the same way we would seek advice from a doctor if we had a niggling health concern, the best way for an SME to overcome doubts and concerns about any aspect of technology is to get advice.

From determining specific technology requirements to identifying key concerns and how to overcome them, an IT advisor can prove invaluable in helping a company analyse and weigh up the cost and potential benefits of IT investments.

Like with any business investment, business owners will need to calculate the return on investment (ROI) when they build a technology plan. An IT advisor will be able to help an SME calculate the ROI on any IT investments it decides to make and identify the efficiencies that they may expect to gain from the investment.

Seeking advice from an expert will also help a small to medium-sized enterprise recognise any gaps, flaws or redundancies in their technology strategy. In some cases, an IT expert will also be able to give a competitive advantage by outlining the benefits of IT investment, present pros and cons of particular systems and even in some cases, discuss which systems competitors are using.

Although a technology plan should be tailor-made to cater for a business's specific requirements, it is also a good idea to know what models competitors are utilising and a good IT advisor will have such knowledge and be in a position to share it.

As technology is gradually being integrated into almost every element of business operations, if a company does not feel it has the adequate knowledge or qualifications to materialise a solid IT integration, it could prove prudent to seek the advice of a professional. IT advisors can help ensure that an SME is not left behind when it comes to the latest hardware, software and other IT equipment. Consulting business and IT solution providers will open up the different possibilities and solutions of how a company can streamline processes in order to improve productivity within the workforce.

Business and IT solution providers and specialists will be able to cast another all-important eye over a business's existing IT infrastructure. In order to improve the operations of a business, it is a good idea to have an outsider who is an expert in the field of technology and communications, to examine the profile of a company from a different perspective.

Carrying out a quick Google search on 'IT advisors' will locate independent consultants both locally and remotely. Alternatively, government agencies can provide useful business and financial advice for SMEs. Local business libraries and enterprise agencies will also be able to offer support on who to turn to for advice on any issues a company may have about technology.

Business start up courses will also provide advice about every aspect of starting a business. From financing the enterprise to recruiting staff and implementing the right kind of technology, business start up courses can be invaluable in helping a start up evolve from a mere business idea to a successful and expanding enterprise.

PART ONE

INFRASTRUCTURE SYSTEMS & SERVICES

INTRODUCTION

This chapter of the eBook will cover the basic infrastructural systems and services that businesses need in order to thrive in the digital environment we now live in. There will be advice for businesses looking to implement these kinds of innovations within their own organisation, as well as information on the benefits and potential advantages that installing this hardware and software can offer for an SME. A combination of hardware and software, the systems covered in this chapter, will outline the very foundation of any business, from security software to lead generation.

The first section will cover a Technology Needs Analysis (or a TND), which is a crucial tool in deciding what direction to move in with regards to hardware and software. This section of the chapter will provide detailed steps on how to perform a TND for any business, large or small, and will offer hints and tips on how to get the very best results out of the assessment process. The assessment process is crucial to the overall success of new systems within the workplace, so following this handy guide will go a long way to ensuring accuracy and quality in the analysis and the new systems.

After TNDs, advice on automated systems follows. With the advance of digital technology, automation has become a staple in many workplaces, and this section will cover the basic automated systems which can assist with everything from email marketing to lead generation and nurturing. Automation can help to free up plenty of time for business owners to grow their prospects, so the information within this section will be especially of use to those looking to expand in the future.

Any business looking to implement a networking system on which to conduct their business must install access management systems to prevent unauthorised persons from gaining access to sensitive information. The next section of the book provides a detailed guide on how to achieve this, with the basic functions of any standard access management tool for a business.

Once access limitations have been established, other network monitoring systems should be put in place. Network management systems help to detect failures or errors within the hardware of a network, and can pinpoint faults in connections or devices which can then be rectified easily and quickly. They also allow for monitoring bandwidth and usage, which is vital for small businesses looking to cut down on their usage; this section will offer helpful tips on what to look for in a network monitoring system.

Lastly, the chapter will cover digital surveillance systems, which are crucial in the protection of sensitive data and securing networks against malicious threats.

This section will look at how digital surveillance systems work against hackers and other threats, as well as looking at the ways they ensure that important data is not stolen and there are no digital intruders.

COMING UP:

- ◥ Technology Needs Analysis

- ◥ Automated Systems

- ◥ Access management systems

- ◥ Network management systems

- ◥ Digital surveillance systems

1

TECHNOLOGY NEEDS ASSESSMENT – WHAT ARE THEY? HOW ARE THEY PERFORMED? DO I NEED ONE?

When attempting to decipher what hardware and software to invest in, an enterprise should take many different elements into consideration. This can be a complicated process for SMEs, but there is an answer in the form of a simple assessment.

A Technology Needs Assessment, sometimes known as a TNA, is primarily written to provide business owners with the basic information that will influence their technology investment decisions. It examines the technology needs and demands of the business and documents the findings in a simple form so that the strategy for investing in hardware and software can be planned in writing.

In order to carry out a thorough Technology Needs Assessment, you will firstly need access to all site staff, all site technology, and a level of documentation capability, as well a connection to the internet. Without access to one of these crucial elements, the findings of the assessment will not be nearly as accurate.

- The person carrying out the assessment should commence by surveying and making detailed documentation of all the existing technology at the site of the business or organisation. This in-depth survey offers a comprehensive view of all existing hardware and software. When recording hardware, it is important to note its age and the condition it is in, whilst with software, update patches, release versions and product keys should all be noted. Both elements of the document should refer to the business processes which the technology facilitates, and the survey needs to be extensive and accurate.

- The next step in the process is to identify where the deficiencies are in this existing technology. Where is the technology failing? Is there more that a certain piece of hardware could do? Is a certain piece of software severely lacking? Some of these issues will have emerged during the first step, and should be very apparent to the person doing the survey.

- It is useful at this point to interview those who use the technology to get their point of view on the state of their technology systems. Interviewing all members of staff can help to expose all the different ways in which the technology is failing, and they are the best placed to make recommendations about suggested improvements, as they will be the ones who use the technology regularly. Make a note of all perceived deficiencies in detail.

- Next, it is time to research the solutions to all of these deficiencies. Does the software across the entire site need upgrading to a newer version? Are the business hardware solutions woefully out of date? Some in-depth research and extensive knowledge on each subject will be required for this step, but it will hopefully hold the key to implementing high-quality hardware and software throughout a workplace.

- In the vast majority of cases where a Technology Needs Analysis is taking place, there will be at least some room for improvement, and hardware, for the most part, is relatively simple to upgrade. Software, however, is slightly different, due to the fact that some updates are not as successful as their predecessors. Become acquainted with online forums, consult some experts and amass some opinions regarding versions and upgrades, to see which would best suit the company needs.

- Seek out some products and start to make comparisons. Which offer the best package deal for a whole workplace? Are there insurance deals and warranties included? Are they sustainable solutions for a business looking to a green future?

- In order to complete the Technology Needs Assessment, all of the findings of this research must be written up in a thorough and comprehensive document, which includes the original survey, the detailed list of deficiencies, along with the list of recommendations for upgrades, with as much accuracy and information as possible. Supporting rationale should be provided wherever necessary, and the estimated cost of such improvements should be calculated.

- Remember when totalling the overall price of technology, to include implementation and support costs that might have been originally overlooked. Maintenance and support for new hardware and software will be ongoing for the entire lifespan of the product, so it is important to factor this into the assessment, as well as the price to purchase the product.

A Technology Needs Assessment is a crucial piece of documentation for any SME looking to upgrade and grow with the help of their hardware and software.

When the above steps have been completed and research conducted, the complete assessment becomes an invaluable strategic tool and IT roadmap. It will be used and referred to regularly, from meetings with sponsors or shareholders who require detailed explanations about expenditure, infrastructure and data security through to making a business case for investing in new technology.

The completed Technology Needs Assessment is also an integral document which can set out when the technology should be purchased and when and how it can be implemented. This is particularly useful if new systems are to be rolled out in phases or over a period of weeks or months.

Expert Opinion: SME Technology Decision Making Framework

Steve Hilton, Principal Analyst at US firm Analysys Mason suggests that SMEs should rely on a four-step decision making process.

- Recognition of a business challenge

- Selection of a trusted technology advisor, via a sales and support channel

- Identification of a technology delivery model

- Selection of a solution

SME technology decision-making framework [Source: Analysys Mason, 2012]

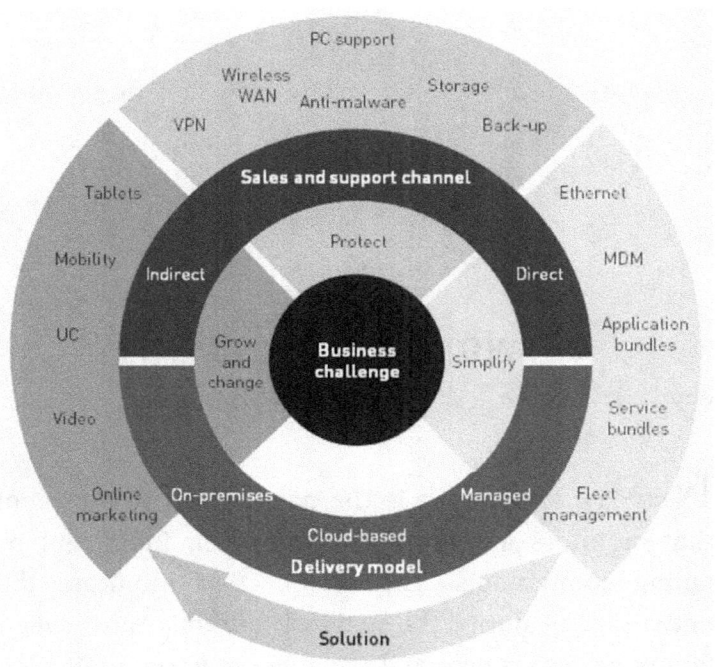

2

NETWORK MANAGEMENT SOFTWARE FOR SMES

Network Monitoring is the name given to a system that monitors a computer network for inefficient or failing components. The system that monitors the network will notify the network administrator when failure or outage occurs. The act of network monitoring is usually carried out by a software application. These can be bought 'off shelf' but can also be built specifically for a particular network.

Network monitoring systems were previously largely used only in corporate and university IT networks; but with workplaces across the globe becoming increasingly oriented towards digital operations, they are starting to become fixtures in SMEs.

A network monitoring system can detect and report the failures or malfunction of any connections or devices within the network. It achieves this goal by sending messages through the network to hosts within the system; the system then verifies the responsiveness of the host, and if the response was unsatisfactorily slow or corrupt, alerts can be sent to certain servers, addresses or phone numbers. This notifies system administrators that there is an issue within their network, and gives them the relevant information they need to fix the problem.

Small businesses need IT networks for all of their daily processes nowadays; every day, 8 petabytes of new information are created across the world, and a percentage of this data is stored within these company networks. Businesses then rely on network management software in order to protect their important data from damage, errors and other potential corruptions, and also to ensure that those accessing the data can do so efficiently and without problems.

Network management software has three main areas, the first of which being availability monitoring. This is the main function which detects any slowness within the system or the routers, and automatically sends a message to the relevant administrator.

The second function that network management software performs is network availability monitoring. This feature keeps tabs on the up and downtimes of servers and systems, allowing administrators to create reports and control Service Level Agreements (SLAs).

Usage management is the third feature of the software. This element tracks how much bandwidth is being consumed by applications, servers and users, so that if there is a performance issue, it can be traced back to the place where the most bandwidth or disk space is being used. Multiple parameters can be tracked, including port numbers and IP addresses, to ensure accuracy in the findings of this monitoring system.

Network monitoring across a whole system of computers and servers is crucial for a business of any size, whether it is a large corporation or a smaller local business. There is greater efficiency through a more advanced level of monitoring; systems completely avoid bandwidth and performance bottlenecks, and sudden surges in bandwidth due to malicious code can be quickly identified and dealt with.

Companies can also reduce their costs significantly by paying close attention to the amount of hardware and bandwidth that they are using on a daily basis. If they find they are not hitting anywhere near their capacity, they can downsize their systems for more cost-effective operation, or they can identify the programs or servers using the most bandwidth and restrict access to them.

Choosing the right monitoring tools helps businesses to reduce their inefficiency and minimise downtime whilst they find the source of errors and failures. With a good networking monitoring system, there will be no more undetected system failures that shut down the entire network for hours while they are fixed.

As a direct result of less downtime, customer satisfaction is improved. The more reliable the system is, the better served customers will be, and the more impressed they will be with the service they receive.

The constant monitoring software also gives administrators and managers peace of mind that their systems are functioning as they should be. As long as there are no alerts, they can rest assured that their systems are working perfectly and performing all the tasks that are asked of them by their team of staff.

3

DIGITAL SURVEILLANCE AND SECURITY FOR SMES

In a world filled with firewalls and complex antivirus systems, it can be tempting for small businesses to buy a basic package and assume that they are protected from malicious threats. Unfortunately in an environment where computer viruses and threats are changing by the day, if not the hour, this is often not the case; simple packages are no longer sufficient for businesses which carry sensitive data within and across their networks.

Many of the conventional antivirus systems will miss plenty of the malware that can target business systems, and they do not offer any protection against targeted attacks. Antivirus systems can only provide a cure, they cannot offer the prevention needed to protect many networks; they can only expel viruses from systems once they have become infected and established what the nature of the virus is.

A system of constant surveillance is thus required to keep businesses safe and secure. Attackers nowadays do not leave incriminating evidence; they are highly trained computer hackers and experts with the know-how to break into many encrypted areas. They will only be caught if a complex system of comprehensive digital surveillance is implemented.

Intruders within networks nowadays, with the creation and exchange of data becoming such a highly prized commodity, can often be more damaging than an intruder on a business premises. Digital targets can be accessed from anywhere in the world, and the threat is far more wide-reaching than the local area, where windows and doors can be locked and physical security installed. More and more businesses are now realising that complete digital surveillance and monitoring of their digital assets is crucial to their success as an organisation.

If intrusions within digital systems aren't detected and stopped quickly and efficiently when they occur, it can have dire consequences for the whole company.

Malicious hackers can leak sensitive information to the public or to competitors and cause huge issues for companies, whilst interruptions to IT systems whilst administrators and technicians attempt to plug the gaps can be costly with regards to both time and money.

An intrusion on a large scale can mean terrible PR for a firm, who may lose clients' trust in them at the same time.

There is also the risk of blackmail, extortion and other criminal activity when a malicious hacker gains entry to a network because of insufficient digital surveillance systems. They can threaten to distribute sensitive or copyrighted material, or even steal from business funds, if they stumble upon the passwords and information associated with company banks accounts.

The solution is to install a fully transparent, comprehensive system of surveillance that monitors all IT security across a network. Network traffic and logs from IT systems flag up attacks and potential intrusions, whilst alarms and alerts from the other integrated systems are monitored by experts at all times. Suspicious looking activity can be acted upon quickly and efficiently to remedy the problem before it escalates into a serious threat.

All systems across this complex software can be managed from a central point, including firewalls, web proxies, authentication gateways and antivirus systems. The monitoring devices which take care of these logs can be managed and updated on a daily basis, and do not disturb the IT environment as a whole. They do not block any access to potentially threatening areas or sites but simply flag up the threat for future follow-ups.

The cost of carrying out this digital surveillance manually would require the employment of at least three extra staff members: this is something that not all small businesses can afford to invest in.

Installing such a system also eliminates the need to trawl jobs boards for highly trained security specialists; this type of software is a 24-hour security specialist in itself, which can help to protect all small business systems from malicious or potentially dangerous external threats.

Monitoring, analysing, recovering and managing data is intrinsic to the overall security and profitability of any

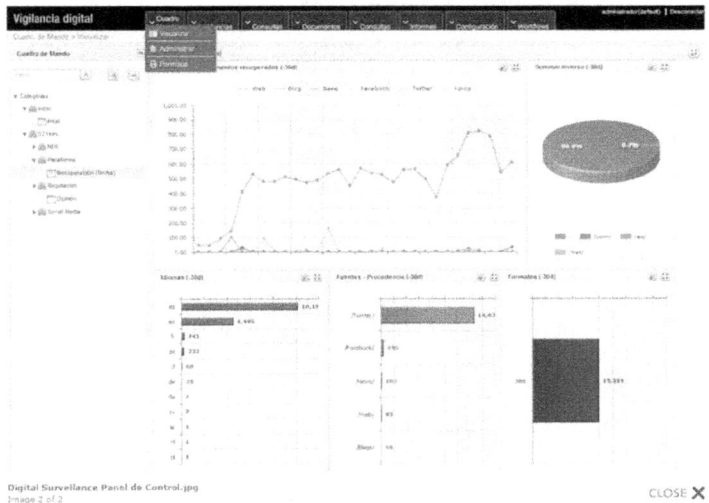

Example of a digital surveillance control panel (source: http://www.s21sec.com/en/technology/digital-surveillance*)*

Expert Opinion

The technology company S21 Sec defines the uses and benefits of digital surveillance systems as:

- Corporate risk management: Protect strategic information assets, monitor information about senior management across the Web, competitive analysis and business intelligence.

- Prevention and mitigation of fraud: Early detection and management of piracy and online fraud, distribution channel monitoring, protection of intellectual and industrial property.

- Detection and monitoring of the volume and sentiment of online mentions and the potential impact on the brand, company or critical assets.

- Protection of critical infrastructures: Critical information monitoring and protection against undesirable actions.

- Information security and brand monitoring: Control of information leaks

- Strategic positioning
    - Competitive intelligence
    - Market analysis
    - Trademark protection.
    - Opinion analysis

4

ACCESS MANAGEMENT AND CONTROL SYSTEMS FOR SMES – GET PROTECTED, NOW

The role of access management software in a business is a very simple one. Before these systems were introduced into businesses, a human would act as a gatekeeper to sensitive information. The access management software allows this person to be removed from the process without losing the access control that keeps information secure.

Many businesses struggle with implementing this software within their company; there are often complications with the classification of information and certain decisions which must be explicitly programmed to deal with certain algorithms.

When responsibility is removed from human hands, there are a great number of safeguards which must be implemented in their place. If a manager wants to access the current salary or previous employment history of an employee at a lower level of seniority, they should be authorised to access this information. However, systems need to be in place to make sure that the lower-placed employee cannot access the private information of their boss. If a human was handling this request, it would be quite simple for them to handle it, but for an access management system, certain safeguards need to be in place to protect sensitive information.

It should be up to the business as a whole rather than a specific IT department to manage the access governance and identity management within their company. The entire process can be a prolonged one, but it is worth it for the ease of use when the systems are finally in place.

Setting up these access management systems require not just the initial assessment, planning and implementation, they also require constant auditing, monitoring and updating to ensure that both the information stored on them and the account access data is up to date.

Providing employees with the appropriate access to certain information and programs within work systems can be done with the relevant software and can reduce the burden on IT departments or outsourced suppliers of IT management.

Through access certification, continuous access governance and role management, access control systems allow businesses a heightened level of visibility and control, which is necessary within SMEs. They can better understand what they have within their working online environment, and who has access to it; they can certify access according to employee entitlement and ensure that every individual has the appropriate access to do nothing more than the job they are employed to do, with no superfluous information leaking through.

Identity administration is a crucial element of access management for SMEs; it allows business owners to better monitor the day-to-day management of all users given access to their systems. Components such as password management, multifactor authentication and single sign-on should all be implemented within the identity administration software, to ensure that associated accounts and identities are only afforded the access that they are entitled to.

The idea that certain employees are entitled to view certain data that others aren't brings into prominence the idea of privileges for certain accounts. It is important for an SME to audit administrative access extensively; privileged credentials should be accompanied by such features as keystroke logging, session audits, policy-based control options that will vary between workplaces, and automated workflows that keep employees productive and on task.

Implementing these privilege systems within a workplace grants administrators only the access they need; nothing more, and nothing less. All activity is tracked, recorded and audited by those who need to know what their employees are up to, and security and compliance is increased across the board.

If administrator accounts are monitored, all user accounts should also experience some level of monitoring. User activity monitoring facilitates security crises responses, where senior members of staff can report on security incidents and any breaches which may occur with accuracy and speed. If users have inappropriate access, this monitoring will help to flag it up and shut it down as soon as possible, whilst if any members of staff are violating company policy in their use of the business's systems, they can be tracked and dealt with appropriately and with haste.

PART TWO

INFRASTRUCTURE SYSTEMS & SERVICES

INTRODUCTION

Part two of Infrastructure Systems and Services will cover more of the basic infrastructural demands that a small business in the digital age needs to get to grips with. Sections will cover a multitude of hardware and software systems, and will even include a detailed guide on what to do if disaster strikes. With everything already learned in part one, this section will provide the ultimate hardware and software start-up guide for SMEs, with information about everything from data systems to internet connections.

The first section covers the essentials surrounding network architecture and design. The design of a communications network for an SME is crucial to their smooth and successful operation, and this section of the guide offers advice on how to achieve a high level of functionality whilst still falling under the cost-effective bracket that many small businesses find themselves in. Covering the functional organisation of the system and the configuration of physical components, the network architecture and design guide will create the ideal small business communications network.

The next part of the chapter covers what to do in the event of a disaster. Whether this is a natural disaster or something else entirely, every business large and small needs to know exactly how they will continue to operate in the face of such high adversity. The 'Disaster Recovery Plan' must be comprehensively formed, to outline how recovery from disaster will be achieved, and to ensure that all members of staff know their role and how they should operate in the case of such situations.

Unified Communication and VoIP is the next section. This covers the new business demand for constant communication, and talks in detail about the UC and VoIP communication solutions. UC brings together a range of communicative methods and allows users to interact using one simple interface; video messages are stored with faxes, emails can be sent along with audio clips, and so on. VoIP is an element of UC, but this section of the book also explains the crucial difference between the two.

We have all heard of the Information Superhighway; this section of the guide offers advice for small businesses looking to connect themselves up to it. Internet service providers often have a range of services and connection types for businesses to choose from, and this section also outlines terms such as 'bandwidth' and 'wideband'. The internet is probably the most crucial tool of all in operating a successful business in the 21st century, so this section is particularly important.

Finally, this section covers the vital design of a company data centre. Data centres form the foundation of a business network and its resources, and they need to have space to grow and expand as our data demands across the world increase by the day.

This section of the book offers expert advice on how to turn architectural design ideas into technological systems which can then be implemented to create a cohesive and effective data centre for a small business.

So, read on and soak up the information provided. It might help your business to become more powerful and it may offer advice for bolstering your foundations.

COMING UP:

- ◤ Network Architecture & Design
- ◤ Unified Communication and VoIP
- ◤ Disaster Recovery & Business Continuity
- ◤ Information Highway: Connecting to the Internet
- ◤ Data centre design, build & operation

1

NETWORK ARCHITECTURE AND DESIGN – YOUR SMALL BUSINESS COMMUNICATIONS NETWORK

Network architecture is essentially the design of a communications network for a small business. This framework operates as a specification of the network's functional organisation and configuration of physical components, as well as the different data formats which are used throughout the network.

The typical small business network includes around one or two dozen computers, a server or two, some networked printers and some access to other networks, such as the internet, for example. These networks need to have the highest level of functionality and be cost-effective to achieve budget ideals.

Before the design of a network commences, it is important that a clear sense of the intended aims are established:

- What must this network accomplish?

- What tasks must it perform on behalf of individuals?

Network design demands a complete assessment of expected functionality beforehand, so examining which tasks will be automated, which business applications will be supported and how much shared access will be necessary, is vital before starting the design process.

Once all of these aspects have been decided, assign priorities to them and begin to deploy the plan. For a functional and effective communications network within the business, take care of essential business functions first and add the finishing touches later..

It is important to have an idea beforehand of the expected size of the network. This is easily calculated when taking into account the number of users and how much they will be accessing the network. Ensure that future growth is also considered and add the facility to bring in more capacity from the very beginning, or you may face issues further down the line. Data storage needs are growing every day, so it is important to design a network that can easily grow in the future.

Use industry-standard components to create the small business network. You never know when you may need to link one network with another, and building a network that is too innovative and not compatible with others of its kind will likely pose problems further down the line. This is especially relevant if your company is an independent brand within a larger organisation, which may demand that the networks unite in the future.

Consider these connectivity issues:

- How much bandwidth will be required?

- Will there need to be a facility to connect with private networks to obtain work from other computers?

These elements of the design process are very complex and will need a lot of thought from both the designers and those who will be making use of the system when it is complete.

Once all functional requirements have been assessed, the real design work can begin. Each network design involves layers, which feed the layers above them and receive information from the layers below. Decisions will need to be made on network types, physical networks, communications equipment and server hardware.

The client will need to choose a network operating system too; Microsoft Windows NT server and Novell NetWare are popular examples of networking operating systems that work well for smaller businesses. Backup hardware and software needs to be bought and configured to ensure that regular backups of the entire network's data will take place and safeguard against corruption or data loss.

Client workstations also need to be considered:

- What type of hardware will be chosen?

- Will you opt for PC or Mac?

- Which operating system offers the best value and the highest standard of business functionality?

Having the aforementioned functional requirement assessments on hand at this stage in the process is integral to making the right decisions and creating a communications network that fits the needs of the business in question.

2

UNIFIED COMMUNICATION AND VOIP

Unified Communication is best defined as a new technological communication solution which bridges the gap between VoIP (Video over IP) and other communication technologies such as instant message and email. It is known as a step forwards from simply using IP-based voice communication to creating a more immersive method of communication which is incredibly useful for small businesses.

Unified Communications, often known as UC, offers a great deal more benefits than VoIP, and brings together a variety of different forms of communication which sets no store by time, device or location.

UC integrates a huge number of different types of communication and organises them within a common interface. These different methods include faxes, emails, voice messages, instant messages and video clips. All forms of communication are delivered to a unified inbox, improving and enhancing the way that businesses interact not only with one another, but also with their clients.

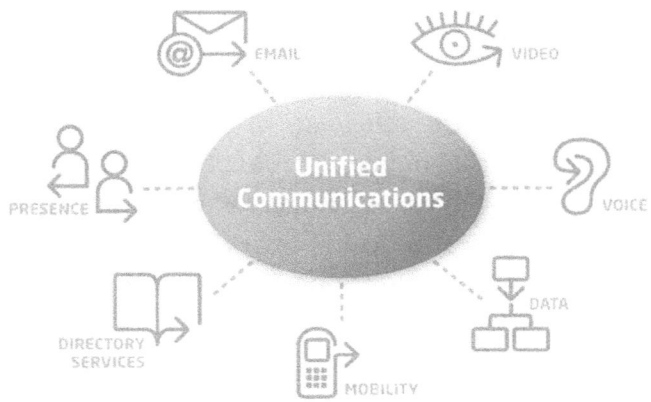

Source: http://blog.coherecomm.com/

There are a great number of ways in which UC systems can be integrated into a small business for a relatively small price. Businesses can now access their faxes and messages left via voicemail simply by logging into their e-mail client; this is an example of UC in one of its simpler forms. More advanced uses of the technology include having emails or faxes read down a phone line, for the recipient to dictate something back which will then be sent as text.

VoIP doesn't necessarily have to be in place already to reap the benefits of UC. Regular phone systems work just fine in implementing a UC system, although previous VoIP systems do make it easier. For instance, businesses which have already made use of a VoIP system will already have the mechanisms in place for forwarding voicemails to email inboxes, and other such features. The scalability is also better if VoIP is involved in the system, rather than just UC products which rely on phone services.

UC in a business and enterprise environment is a huge leap for many. The initial implementation can be costly, but it reduces operational costs in the long run and streamlines the efficiency of a business. Many of the standards can increase productivity dramatically, particularly in the types of companies that frequently rely on communications, either with partner companies, vendors, clients or other members of staff within that company.

UC systems allow employees to carry out a high standard of communication across a range of platforms with ease and simplicity. They can access their emails, voice messages and faxes without having to change devices. For example, emails are usually handled on computers, voice messages are sent through telephones and faxes go straight to fax machines: however, this is not the case with a UC system, which sends them all to one consistent interface, usually on a computer. If employees can receive messages in such a way, it follows that they can also respond to them. They do not need to exit the messaging system to send another message, to forward emails to someone whilst in a call or to read a fax whilst sending a voice message.

Messages can be sent to multiple recipients by making a single phone call, and email messages can be dictated over the phone. Fax messages can be viewed in email clients on mobile devices, and they can also be sent as email attachments to colleagues or partners. Notifications are also integrated into one system, which means that whether someone receives a video message, an email or an instant message, they will be notified on their computer or their mobile phone.

Users are offered a higher level of control over the calls they accept. They can screen their calls before they are taken, sending less crucial calls to the voicemail system, which they can then access with ease.

With VoIP being widely adopted in many workplaces, it is making the switch to UC much easier. The two technologies complement each other perfectly, and whilst they can work perfectly competently apart, they perform better when working in tandem with one another, and offer a host of business benefits to the growing SME.

Expert Opinion: Peter Alexander, Cisco Systems Inc

In a 2005 article for Entrepreneur.com, Peter Alexander of Cisco Systems Inc. identified the main business benefits of VOIP as:

1. The quality of service offered by VOIP has improved since the technology was first incepted.

2. VoIP can significantly reduce telecommunications costs

3. VoIP makes phone systems highly flexible as the phone system can go where the worker does, increasing productivity.

Read the full article here: http://www.entrepreneur. com/article/79842

Company Budgets

Budgets are naturally an integral component of running a business. Not only does setting budgets and adhering to them mean that companies are more likely to be profitable, but they also serve as a plan of action for business owners, directors and managers. Budgets also provide a point of comparison at the end of a financial period.

It is important to remember that business budgets work considerably differently to household budgets. While household budgets typically comprise of allocating various expenditures within a specific income, there is a lot more involved with business budgets.

A company should use a budget to effectively determine its spending performance. As *Investopedia* cites, in the business world "the ability to gauge performance using budgets is a matter of life or death."

A companies' static budget comprises of numbers based on expected outputs and inputs for each of the business's departments. A static budget is widely seen as a guideline, the first part of the budgeting process that determines how much a company has and how much it will spend.

Relying solely on a static budget can cause problems when it comes to an unforeseen expenditure occurring. Let's take unforeseen disasters in technology as an example here.

Research by the highly respected David Lewis Consultancy concluded in a comprehensive study that 70% of businesses are most concerned with cost when investing in technology. Expenditure was cited as the most important consideration and the strongest influencer on which technology was purchased. Significantly 80% of respondents also agreed that technology innovation and new business solutions were both strategic and vital to the growth and competitive success of smaller enterprises.

According to data compiled by Spiceworks, as of March 2013, the amount of money small- and medium-sized businesses are spending on technology is increasing. Spicework's latest State of SMB IT report suggests that during the first half of 2013, SMEs budgets increased by 19%, which is the biggest budget increase during the last three years. This increase was most pronounced among smaller companies, typically with 250 employees or less.

The data, which represented the opinions of more than 1,000 IT professionals, most of which from North America, revealed that hardware claimed the biggest portion of IT budgets, with tablet computers showing the biggest increase. Approximately 61% of the SMEs that participated in the survey admitted that they used at least one cloud service. Smaller companies, with 20 employees or less, are the most likely to install cloud services. What's more, these companies spend almost 19% of their budgets on such services. The survey also revealed that 72% of the respondents said that they had invested in server virtualisation.

The survey attests that modern-day SMEs are increasingly dedicating a larger chunk of their budget to technology such as cloud services. In our quest to implement advanced and innovative technology in order to improve business operations and increase productivity, business contingency planning needs to be in operation in order for companies to avoid being monetarily frozen should an IT disaster occur.

By avoiding to implement a contingency plan, SMEs are putting themselves at risk from not being able to financially cope should an IT disaster occur. It is therefore imperative that SMEs move beyond the static budget model and employ a more flexible budget approach. A flexible budget is essentially a budget that includes figures that are based on actual output. At the end of a financial period, it is time for a company to see whether it adhered to its planned expenditures. This is when a flexible budget is used. The enterprise's actual output is compared to its static budget to enable business owners to have a clearer picture of the differences between what level of spending was expected and what actually occurred.

The flexible budget will therefore be a true representation of expenditures, including what may have been spent on IT and IT disaster recovery strategies. This will ultimately mean that a company will have a clearer picture of what they may need to budget for in the next financial period.

The next question is how much an SME should spend on disaster recovery. The odds are that a company, no matter how big or small, will eventually require disaster recovery. The basic premise is that an SME should spend the least amount possible to ensure an appropriate level of continuous operations, without spending more than its operations are worth. If, for example, a company makes £100,000 a year, then forking out £100,000 a year on continuous operations capability would not be advisable – for obvious reasons.

However, it would be a wise investment for a company to allocate some budget to ensure that it doesn't lose valuable data, such as client information and accounting statistics. According to a whitepaper provided by Outsource IT Needs:

"A quick and dirty rule of thumb is to use the value your business generates over a one-week period. Take your annual revenue and divide by 52."

This is the total loss a business would experience if it closed its business operations for one week, and it gives us a clearer picture of how much we would lose if an IT disaster affected a company for a week. It also leaves us with a clearer understanding of how much of a business's budget should be allocated to implement a contingency plan.

Expert Opinion: Budgets vary hugely from company to company, country to country

SME Budgeting is still a very personal thing with huge changes within industries and from country to country.

In Great Britain, a Federation of Small Business survey found a major imbalance in SME tech budgets between England and Scotland.

But, over the last year, Scottish small businesses invested less than the UK average on new technology.

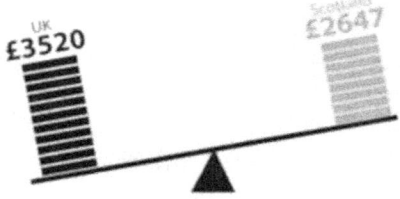

The FSB asked:
"How much have you invested in technologies in the past 12 months?"

Source: http://www.techradar.com/news/world-of-tech/management/scots-trail-in-technology-investment-1150465

Extract from a Business Standard feature on Gujurat SMEs

While their larger counterparts may be going slow on information technology (IT) spending, small and medium enterprises (SMEs) in Gujarat are raising their IT spend. According to IT hardware and software component providers, there has been a 15-20 per cent increase in IT spending among SMEs in the state in the past six months.

"These days, large industries are pretty cautious as far as increasing their IT spending is concerned. However, SMEs are not so prone to global economic upheavals and are growing domestically. Hence, they have increased their expenditure on IT infrastructure in a bid to become more competitive," says K J Thakker, committee member and immediate past president of the Ahmedabad Computer Manufacturers' Association.

Having increased their IT infrastructure budgets, in both hardware and software, a typical SME with sales revenues of Rs 50-100 lakh now spends around Rs 100,000 a year on IT. Further, an SME with a turnover of Rs 5-10 crore spends around Rs 10-12 lakh per year on IT expansion.

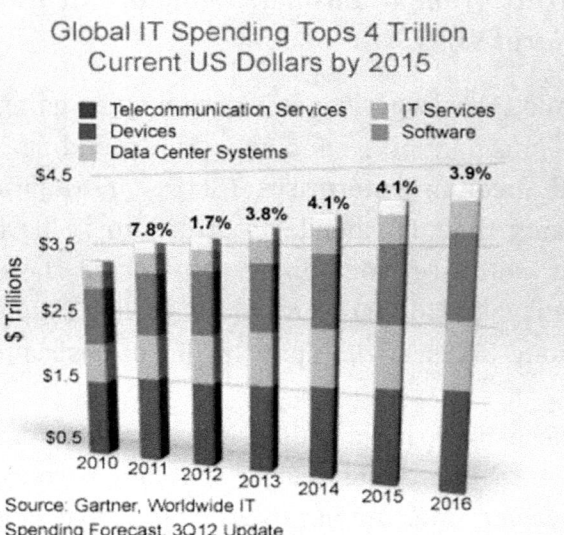

Source: Gartner, Worldwide IT
Spending Forecast, 3Q12 Update

Expert Opinion: Gartner IT Spending Forecast Summary, Q2 2013

- Gartner's forecast for 2013 IT spending growth in U.S. dollars has been reduced from 4.1% in the previous quarter to 2.0% this quarter. This mainly reflects the impact from changes of exchange rates, as growth in constant currency is forecast at 3.5% for 2013, only down slightly from 4.0% the previous quarter. (Source: http://www.gartner.co m)

Of course, while budget is the biggest concern with 70% of businesses indicating that cost is the main factor influencing their choice of technology, other issues must also be considered. Data security is of paramount importance and concern. A Boston Consulting Group report, commissioned in 2013 by Microsoft, found that 60% of small business owners and managers believe that data security and privacy concerns inhibit their adoption of new technologies. The report entitled *Ahead of the Curve: Lessons on Technology and Growth from Small Business Leaders (source: http://www.business-standard.com/article/sme/data-security-smes-top-technology-concern-says-report-113102100935_1.html)* identified the shift towards future technologies such as cloud computing as one of the sources of the concern, with many worried that hacking could be more widespread and that their critical data assets would be less secure if stored in the cloud.

Interestingly, the report also cites the need for more local IT ecosystems, revealing that many small business owners do not feel that they have the necessary IT expertise in house to lead IT acquisition and implementation strategy. This dependence on external suppliers means that a stronger ecosystem of IT experts is needed at local level, to offer guidance and support at the time of purchase and deployment of both hardware and software.

A third issue raised by the report and a growing area of concern for many SME decision makers relating to hardware and software is that of new technologies. With the majority already admitting to lacking the necessary expertise in-house, many fear that this will inhibit their adoption of new technologies, such as cloud computing, due to a lack of resources. The report states that 30% of Indian SME managers for example felt their staff did not have enough of an understanding, skills, training and exposure to IT to make new technology easy.

Duties, taxes and regulations were also raised in the report as areas of concern, with some businesses simply put off new technology adoption because of the cost of compliance.

3

DISASTER RECOVERY AND BUSINESS CONTINUITY – ARE YOU PREPARED?

"As technologies are constantly developing, the implementation of a disaster recovery plan or a high availability system solution can be very complex and costly nowadays in terms of administration of processes and resources as opposed to direct costs of implemented products (hardware, software). Therefore, innovation should be a simplification, consolidation and optimization service in order to reduce administration costs." NEC IT Platform.

It is recommended that all organisations, large and small, should have an emergency plan in place which will be utilised in the event of a disaster.

This 'Disaster Recovery Plan' or 'Business Continuity Plan' will outline how recovery from the event will be achieved, and it is advised that all businesses are all prepared to ensure that they will know how to approach things if disaster should ever strike them.

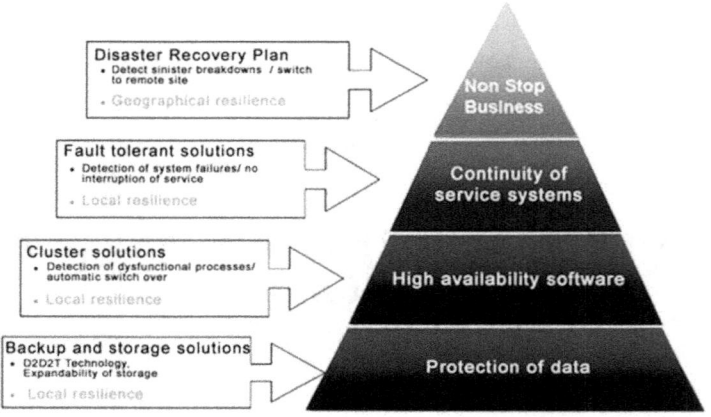

Source: http://www.nec-itplatform.com

Surprisingly, the 2012 SMB Disaster Preparedness Survey found that many SMEs are chronically unprepared for disaster. Just 14% of those surveyed had a disaster recovery plan in place. A worrying 73% of respondents said they knew they were unprepared and would be left wanting if disaster were to strike but simply could not do anything about it. Most cited a lack of resources, with 20% saying they simply did not have what they needed to get a disaster recovery plan in place and 40% complaining of insufficient finance.

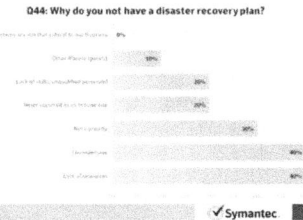
Every organisation, no matter how big or small, is likely to face a disaster at some point. A disaster recovery plan is what stands between a strong reaction and a situation from which there is no recovery. The disaster recovery plan is what sets out the safeguards as to how important documents are protected, what fail-safes there are in place for critical business data and how staff and equipment responds when the unexpected arrives on the doorstep unannounced.

The Disaster Recovery Plan is often established after performing an audit of the recovery capacity that an organisation has. Successful disaster audits state their objectives in an audit plan, and they go a long way to creating the recovery plan for a business.

The first thing that a business should do in developing their plan, is to establish a team of responsible and experienced employees who know the business inside out. They should all be assigned responsibilities for specific disaster-related tasks.

Disaster risks should then be identified:

- Where is your business most at risk?

- What kinds of disasters are most likely to be experienced?

An identification of hazards and risks exercise may look something like this:

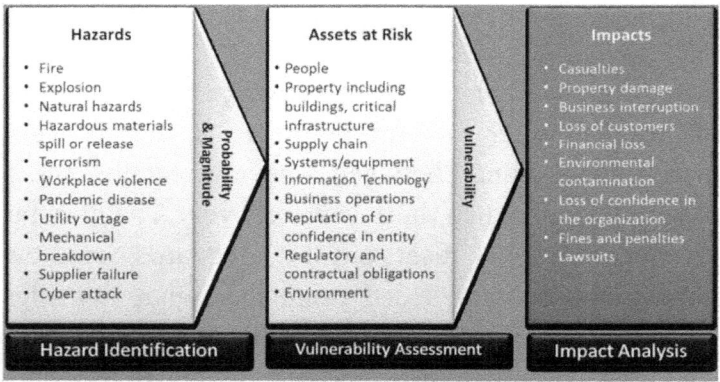

Source: *Ready.gov: http://www.ready.gov/risk-assessment*

It is important to prioritise the critical business functions that allow the organisation to stay in operation, and make sure that in the course of the plan, these functions are the ones recovered first. These plans should be updated at least once a year to deal with ever-changing business structures.

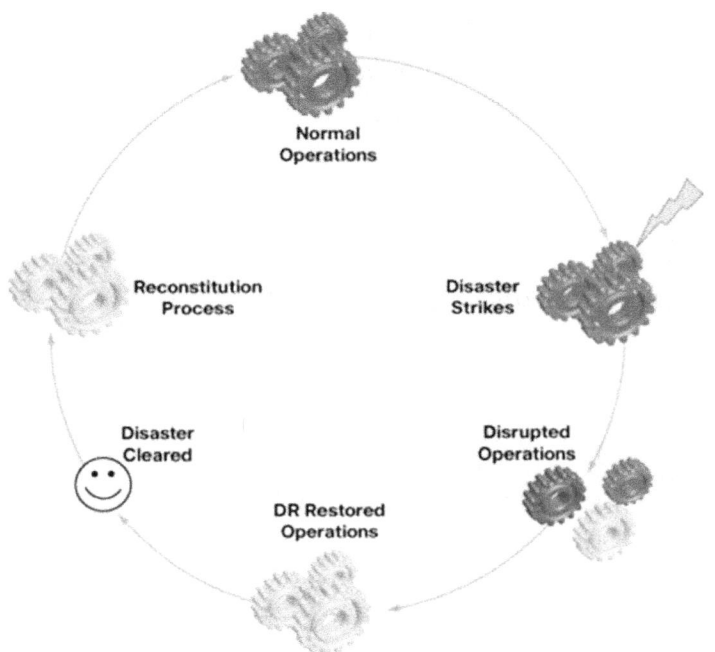

Source: http://www.cisco.com/en/US/technologies/collateral/
tk869/tk769/white_paper_c11-453495.html

If possible, ensure there is another site where employees can work in the event of a disaster, with access to back-up systems and emergency supplies. Establish which locations are available:

- Is there a branch office that could act as headquarters for a short time?

- Could the office of a business partner be viable as a temporary home for the business?

A hotel conference room or even someone's home office could be a useful choice if the business is a relatively small one.

The back-up site should be well equipped to deal with the sudden influx of operations. It should have the relevant computers and software, all of the data files which are needed to ensure the continuous operation of the business (accounts, orders, inventories, etc.), as well as any extra equipment which is necessary.

As part of the Disaster Recovery Plan, there should also be an element of safeguarding for the property;

- Which parts of the property could survive a potential disaster?

- Would it affect the building and the equipment within?

- Would company vehicles be affected?

- If company records are stored on site, are they secure enough to remain intact?

Update contact information regularly as part of a well-maintained Disaster Recovery Plan. This includes all of the email-address and relevant phone numbers for employees, important customers or clients, vendors and insurance companies. Make the contact information easily accessible, to all employees if necessary.

If contact information is up-to-date, it is also important that communication methods are established. There should be a fail-safe, reliable method for employees to communicate with one another; this could be through email, mobile phones, a website or another method of modern communication which is accessible to all.

Prepare all employees and ensure they are fully briefed on what they will need to do in the event that a Disaster Recovery Plan is put into action. Ensure they know where they will relocate to work, ensure they have access to the tools and equipment they need to carry out their jobs, and ensure that they have access to sufficient communication tools to remain on the radar at all times.

In the event that an evacuation, employees should be prepared to grab only the most critical records and equipment they have to hand.

This should include the Business Continuity Plan, any company contracts or insurance policies, a list of all bank accounts and information, and as many customer orders as possible. Secure the building before leaving.

Cash flow will be an issue in the event of a disaster. Try to get hold of credit cards and chequebooks in the event of an evacuation, and have enough cash on hand to take care of any immediate issues. Internet banking can help, and can be carried out using smartphones in this day and age, so access to company accounts should not be an issue and bills will still get paid.

Initiate all post-disaster recovery procedures. Assign specific tasks to the responsible employees designated (as discussed at the start of this section), and track the progress and the effectiveness of the entire plan in the event that something similar should happen again.

Expert Opinion: What are the basics of an IT disaster recovery plan?

Abraham Guerrero is a systems analyst, Microsoft certified professional, technology enthusiast and experienced real estate investor. His guidelines for creating an IT disaster recovery plan, as published on the Yahoo! Contributor network on June 08 2012 are:

- **IT priorities should match business priorities 100%.** In a hypothetical scenario where the entire IT infrastructure is destroyed, who in the business needs to be up and running the soonest? Some might say that the payroll department needs to be the first to be made operational again. Others might say that their building security system is #1. It's important to list all major systems and create a review team to sort the list in order of priority.

- **Establish expectations during the recovery process with an SLA chart.** Determine an appropriate ratio of downtime/cost of fail-over and backup protection is right for your organization. Then list those in a simple chart. For example, you might have a high downtime **tolerate** for an intranet site that lets people schedule the use of a meeting room. However, you might have zero to no downtime tolerance for a system that has to do with safety or securing sensitive areas. This simple SLA template establishes expected availability of systems during the recovery process.

- **Document requirements for insurance claims process.** If safety is not an issue, this may be one of your first steps in the recovery process. If you have damaged equipment, you might need to initiate a claims process against your insurance policy so that you can start the process of obtaining replacement equipment as soon as possible.

- **Establish a restoration procedure.** For a basic recovery plan, the restoration plan does not need to go into intricate details. Some things that are worth putting into the procedure though, are software license keys, warranty information, backup location, administrative passwords, and temporary sites. A printed copy of important passwords should be kept in an off-site safe that is accessible by key management staff. Consider placing it in a bank safety deposit box if appropriate for your situation.

Read the full article here: http://voices.yahoo. com/how-create-simple-disaster-recovery-plan-11416832.html?cat=15

4

THE INFORMATION SUPERHIGHWAY: SMES CONNECTING TO THE INTERNET

The internet has become perhaps the most crucial tool at a small business's disposal. It allows them to connect to a global database of potential clients and then offers unlimited promotional opportunities to open up their client base.

In some cases, business internet use will be determined by location.

Internet World Statistics from 2010 paint a surprising picture, suggesting that Internet penetration, despite explosive growth over the course of the last decade, still hovers at just under 30% globally.

With a lack of investment in infrastructure planning due to socio-politic instability, Africa has just 10% internet penetration, making it the lowest on the planet. This poses a significant challenge for businesses in the region. Elsewhere, 58.4% of the European population is connected to the information superhighway, as is 77.4% of America.

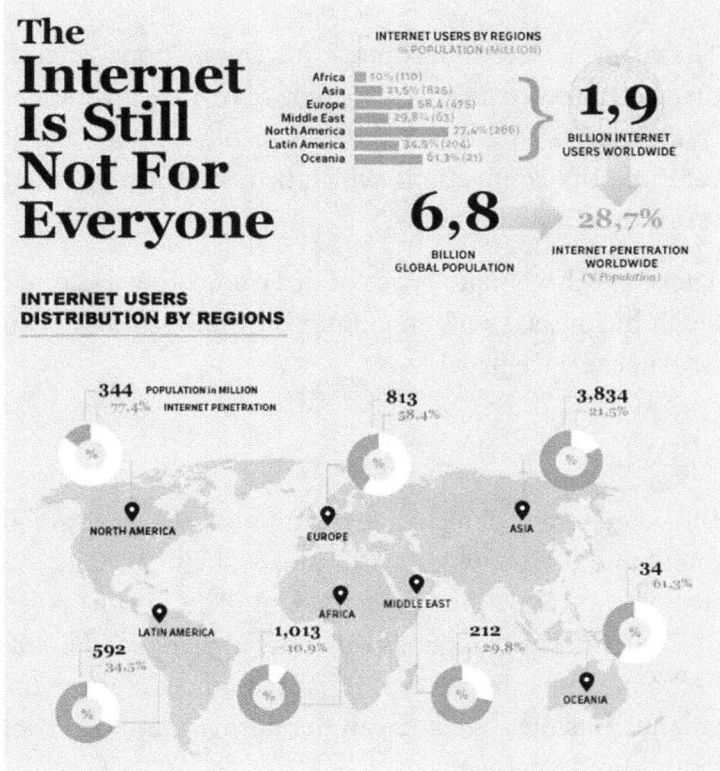

In order to connect to the internet, assuming that all the relevant network hardware and software is in place, SMEs must first determine their internet demands, their needs, and what type of internet connection they will benefit from using.

When browsing for internet access, there is plenty of marketing jargon and lingo that has to be dealt with. 'Broadband' and 'high-speed' are the most commonly used terms to describe any type of internet which provides a higher bandwidth speed than the old-fashioned dial-up access.

These terms are superfluous; all connections offered on the market today are faster than dial-up access. 'Wideband' is quite a new term to be defined, and it refers to the connections which provide throughput at levels of around 50 mbps.

There are three main types of internet connection that small businesses will encounter on their search for an internet service provider.

1. DSL

DSL is generally the cheapest, and uses the traditional telephone lines which will most likely already be installed in the office environment. The performance of DSL internet depends on how far away the ISP exchange hotspot is, but it is a sound solution for smaller businesses as it can support around a dozen users simultaneously.

2. Cable

Cable is the next most common of connection types. The technology works through television cable lines, which might not be installed in an office environment, but are easily fitted. Cable speeds are much faster than DSL speeds, offering between 50 mbps and 100 mbps for downloads. However, cable connections end up sharing their bandwidth allowances with other users in the vicinity, which can lead to slow speeds when everyone logs on at the same time.

3. Fibre-Optic

Fibre-optic is the most modern and most effective connection type. Fibre-optic is currently being rolled out on an extended basis around the world, so if the business is located in a rural area, it might still be a few years before it is installed.

Download speeds can reach around 150 mbps with a fibre-optic connection. Speeds like this can support high bandwidth, multiple users, as well as different services including TV, phone and internet.

Once you have settled on the type of internet connection which will be most suitable for the size and demands of your business, it is recommended that you establish your bandwidth requirements. Choosing a speed which is suitable for the business is one of the key decisions in setting up an entire network, as much of the activity carried out online depends on bandwidth capabilities.

The general rule of thumb is that the more people who will be using the network, the more bandwidth will be required. If those users are performance-heavy, and using applications which contain streaming video, downloading large files or making use of VoIP phones, the bandwidth requirements will be much higher.

Conversely, if the extent of the internet usage for a business doesn't stretch beyond checking emails and using a web browser to check on latest news, business information or for research purposes, you won't need nearly as much bandwidth.

It is worth remembering that some internet service providers do place a cap on data usage to prevent abuse of downloads. Exceeding data limits can result in a surcharge being added to a bill, or all bandwidth being scaled back until the bill is paid. This shouldn't be a problem for most businesses who do not count streaming video and regular downloads among their everyday activities, but it is a point worth bearing in mind.

Internet service providers almost always provide the appropriate equipment for their customers. Business clients have slightly more advanced needs than the typical home set-up, so having a discussion with a representative from the internet company about your business's specific needs is always recommended. Some companies charge installation fees, but many waive the fees depending on the length of a business contract and the amount of custom they are receiving from one client.

Internet service providers usually only install their internet hardware on a single computer, so the responsibility will fall to the business to ensure the internet is ready and raring to go on all of their other devices. There are plenty of guides and instruction manuals online for those struggling with this concept, but it is generally a case of connecting the wires and running a configuration wizard.

Once these steps are complete, a business has the world at their fingertips, quite literally. They have access to the Information Superhighway, and can connect with anyone, anywhere in the world – to sell, to buy or simply to interact.

In a survey carried out by Dalberg Research, 80% of African businesses believe Internet access has the power to improve their business and 70% believe the internet will create jobs if their businesses can get online. This snapshot of SME consciousness in the continent shows just how important connectivity is.

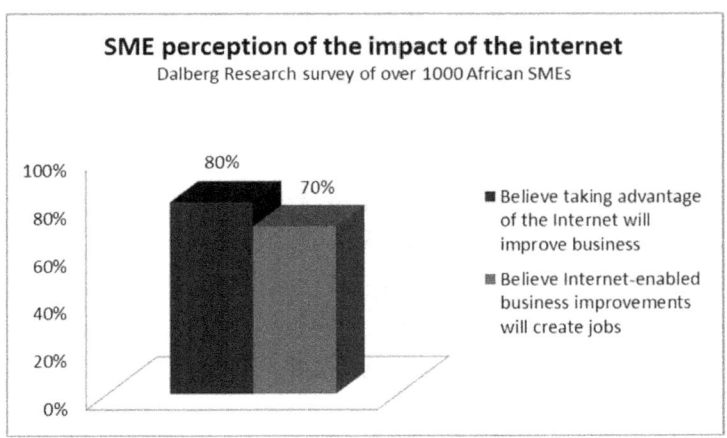

Source: http://dalberg.com/blog/

5

DATA CENTRES: DESIGN, BUILD AND OPERATE

Incredible rates of data growth, a volatile economy and the environmental issues regarding energy usage are all putting substantial pressure on the data centre as an enterprise. In answer to this pressure, virtualization is seen increasingly as the answer – a practical and effective way to reduce costs, simplify management and promote a greener IT department. Virtualizing servers means less hardware is required; which makes the prospect an attractive one for those worried about cost. As there is less equipment to house, and energy consumption is lower with fewer actual servers to power, less physical space is needed.

It is important to get the architecture of the centre perfect; this reduces the risk involved with designing and building such an entity in order to ensure that the centre is future-proofed, efficient and optimised. This can of course be a costly and complicated process.

Expert Opinion: Data Centres

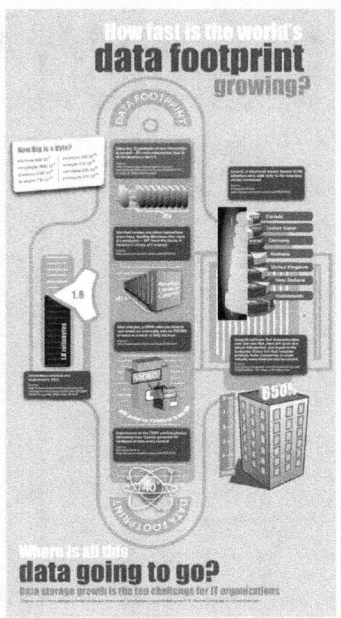

Definition: The data centre is the department in an enterprise that houses and maintains back-end information technology (IT) systems and data stores—its mainframes, servers and databases. In the days of large, centralized IT operations, this department and all the systems resided in one physical place, hence the name data centre.

Several factors are driving enterprises to look beyond traditional technology infrastructure silos and transform the way they view their data centre environment and business processes. These include aging data centre infrastructures that are at risk for not meeting future business requirements, an ongoing cost-consciousness, and the need to be more energy-efficient.

Many enterprises are looking to virtualization, fabric-based infrastructure, modular designs and cloud computing as they explore how best to optimize their resources. Source: Gartner.

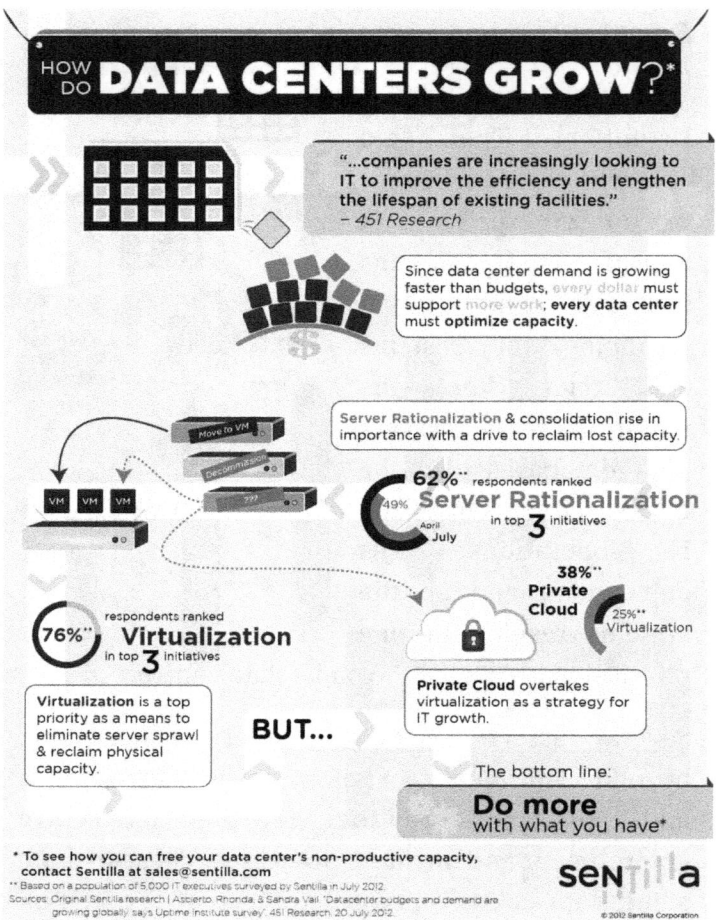

Source: http://blog.ness.com/spl/bid/81674/Consolidating-Data-Center-Infographic

Data centres usually need to address the following issues, so all of these points should be considered as you set about choosing a data centre designer or embark on designing your own data centre infrastructure:

1. **Expense:** They must reduce capital expenses through better management of workloads. They allow company resources to be available at all times, providing flexibility in line with the world's demand for instant information.

2. **Innovation:** They must enable or increase innovation through new models and the adoption of further layers in the network architecture.

3. **Use:** They must improve how assets are utilised in order to reduce or defer capital expenses.

4. **Energy Efficiency:** They should reduce power consumption, cutting the cost of operations and aligning themselves with 'eco-friendly' practices.

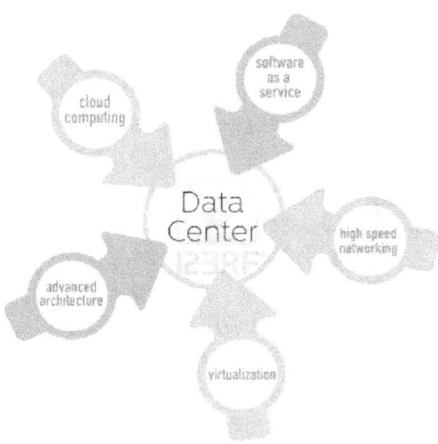

Source: http://www.123rf.com/photo_14232413_cloud-computing-network-architecture-arrows-point-at-data-center-design.html

These specific points allow architects and designers to draw up a set of principles which guarantee that the data centre will confront each challenge. They can then be matched a number of technological requirements to create a blueprint of sorts:

Date Centre Blueprint

Architectural Principles	Technological Requirements
Efficiency	Virtualization of infrastructure with appropriate management tools. Infrastructure homogeneity is driving asset utilization up.
Scalability	Platform scalability can be achieved through explicit protocol choice (for example, TRILL) and hardware selection; and also through implicit system design and implementation.
Reliability	Disaster recovery (BCP) planning, testing, and operational tools (for example, VMware's Site Recovery Manager, SNAP, or Clone backup capabilities).
Interoperability	Web-based (XML) APIs, for example, WSDL (W3C) using SOAP or the conceptually simpler RESTful protocol with standards compliance semantics, for example, RFC 4741 NETCONF or TMForum's Multi-Technology Operations Systems Interface (MTOSI) with message binding to "concrete" endpoint protocols.

Flexibility	Software abstraction to enable policy-based management of the underlying infrastructure. Use of "meta models" (frames, rules, and constraints of how to build infrastructure). Encourage independence rather than interdependence among functional components of the platform.
Modularity	Commonality of the underlying building blocks that can support scale-out and scale-up heterogeneous workload requirements with common integration points (web-based APIs). That is, integrated computer stacks or infrastructure packages (for example, a Vblock or a FlexPod). Programmatic workflows versus script-based workflows (discussed later in this chapter) along with the aforementioned software abstraction help deliver modularity of software tools.
Security	The appropriate countermeasures (tools, systems, processes, and protocols) relative to risk assessment derived from the threat model. Technology countermeasures are systems based, security in depth. Bespoke implementations/design patterns required to meet varied hosted tenant visibility and control requirements necessitated by regulatory compliance.
Robustness	System design and implementation—tools, methods, processes, and people that assist to mitigate collateral damage of a failure or failures internal to the administratively controlled system or even to external service dependencies to ensure service continuity.

Source: http://www.ciscopress.com/articles/article.asp?p=1804857&seqNum=2

Following the architectural guidelines set out in this table allows designers to create a blueprint that they can work from in creating their personalised data centre.

PART THREE

INFRASTRUCTURE SYSTEMS AND SERVICES

INTRODUCTION

Where once business computing was rooted in the tangible – hardware that could be touched, components that could be seen, software that was saved on to a hard disk, a CD-Rom or a floppy disk, modern infrastructures and services are increasingly intangible – that is to say, virtual.

The world has undergone a seismic shift in the last decade, rendering the IT landscape almost unrecognisable. Rather than go to the store and buy a software package in a box, provided on a CD-ROM with a registration key on a sticker, programmes are now provided online, available to download and register with nothing more than an email address.

Where once crime related to the physical theft of a computer, a laptop or a peripheral such as a printer or scanner, this move towards digital infrastructure and virtual systems has led to the rise of so-called cyber crime – an information superhighway along which a new kind of highwayman lurks.

Hackers and spyware, malware and viruses are all now a part of everyday life, common terms that give new meaning to threats to data security, hardware and technology. Where once a hard drive may have faced danger from spilled liquids, floods or fires, today it can be just as easily destroyed by online snoopers.

Along with these changes comes new ways of working. New systems to get to grips with which offer infinite possibilities, new opportunities to maximise efficiency and productivity and seemingly endless ways in which existing systems can be put to work to do bigger and better things.

In a physical world, data would be stored locally or printed out and filed for safe keeping. Today it can be stored in the cloud, a term coined to reflect how sensitive data and business critical information can 'float'. Not only does this reduce the need for SMEs to have storage facilities on site, it also opens up brand new methods of working and easier means of collaboration – a colleague working in one office can now have the same, instant access to a document or data as a colleague in the next room, the next town or even the next country.

Getting to grips with the digital or virtual infrastructure can seem like an impossible task in a world where innovations are made at the speed of light. But, as you'll see when you read through this chapter, it is these advances that present so many opportunities to SMEs.

There are not only cost savings to consider and the ease of collaboration we'll see made possible by cloud computing, but also the convenience of being able to share information virtually ard the myriad marketing and organizational opportunities ensconced within a web presence and web portals.

Of course there are threats to anyone embracing the internet: internet users storing business data online or using mobile computing must be aware of the inherent dangers lurking in this new, digital landscape.

COMING UP:

- ◥ Hardware refresh anc upgrade best practices
- ◥ Web Presence and portals
- ◥ Cyber crime
- ◥ Digital forensics
- ◥ Green computing
- ◥ Mobile computing security
- ◥ Cloud computing

1

HARDWARE REFRESH AND UPGRADE BEST PRACTICES

Just as you need to add a lick of paint to your office walls every now and again and change the tyres on your car when the wear and tear starts to show, so you also need to consider the maintenance of your hardware and refresh or upgrade as needed.

For many businesses, hardware represents a significant financial investment and often, one of the biggest drains on the IT budget. It is also one of the most important areas of business computing, as the right hardware tools can make a dramatic difference as to how effectively the organization as a whole performs. While insufficient memory and an outdated CPU will drag out tasks that should take a few minutes into a frustrating cycle of waiting, more efficient hardware will speed up processes, reduce downtime and help employees to complete their tasks more efficiently and quickly.

It is not overstating the case to suggest that striking the right balance between optimizing the hardware refresh cycle while also cutting costs to keep business finances streamlined, is one of the biggest, most difficult and most fraught responsibilities facing SME owners and managers.

Any business needs to be able to respond quickly when problems arise. It is unthinkable that a need for new IT equipment which will help the business to carry out its work should go unanswered. And yet, without an appropriate hardware refresh schedule in place, this may well be the case.

It is a mistake to think of hardware refresh as simply an extra cost to have to absorb. Implemented correctly, an effective refresh policy can make sure that spend is optimised, decisions are correctly made, appropriate procedures are followed and that avoidable breakdowns and unexpected bills are sidestepped.

An IT hardware refresh does represent a potentially large chunk of annual spending and operating expense. In some cases, depending on hardware needs, it may run into millions of pounds per annum. For this reason, a best practise refresh policy is essential. Even if refresh and upgrade needs are small now, creating a refresh cycle that can be upgraded as the business grows is an advisable means of avoiding problems later.

Archstone Consulting say in their IT effectiveness white paper that,

"An effective refresh policy will guide IT and accounting personnel through the analyses needed to balance the trade-offs between capital spending, operating efficiency, and risk mitigation.

"However, in many companies, the IT refresh decisions don't strike this balance because they are driven by just one parameter -accounting depreciation schedules. Standard 3 and 5-year refresh periods are applied across all IT hardware, leading to unnecessary spending in some areas and unplanned risk of failure in others."

Putting a hardware refresh policy together means developing a systematic and cohesive approach. It must consider not only useful life lifecycles and account depreciation schedules but also look at how savings in operating costs and labour can be achieved.

You can create a formal or informal hardware refresh and upgrade policy but the important thing is that you do create one. This single document will ensure that you make the most of technological advances, get the best return on existing equipment and avoid unnecessary downtime through avoidable hardware failure.

What's Included in a Hardware Refresh and Upgrade Policy?

A hardware refresh and upgrade policy should contain two distinct sections for complete clarity of purpose:

- Section 1: Type of hardware under consideration.

- Section 2: Timescales or period in years before hardware must be refreshed or upgraded.

The primary purpose of your hardware refresh and upgrade best practise policy is to safeguard your organisation. This important document means that you avoid placing your company at the risk of running, using and relying upon old and or unsupported components.

The single most important consideration to ponder when creating a hardware refresh policy is your business and its technology requirements. Your policy should consider average use times, amount of wear and tear placed upon components and their importance in your organization as a whole. If you are a web design agency and produce video content for clients, the graphic cards and perhaps web cams will be important. If you're an accountant, your hard drive and its ability to run potentially more demanding applications as they become available is paramount. If you're a photographer, your monitor is your digital eye – the clarity of the display and the ports on your tower, its ability to accept memory cards from new digital cameras or other technologies must be considered. In each of these cases, you cannot risk putting off an upgrade because your account depreciation schedule calls for a five year useful life period, if you know your hardware will be rendered obsolete in three.

If your refresh policy has not been developed with day-to-day practicalities in mind, it places you at risk of not being able to take full advantage of your refresh spend and may mean you are missing out on available savings.

Do not fall into the all-to-easy trap of having a blanket guideline that states hardware refresh will take place across the board every four years. Each piece of equipment must be assessed individually – a keyboard may last several years after that self-imposed refresh line, whereas a disk storage system may be struggling after three. A monitor may work OK after five years but it may lack energy saving technology which could deliver lower power consumption benefits.

Savings in hardware spending as a result of too lax a refresh policy should not be confused with savings across the board. If you do not familiarise yourself with the optimal working lifecycle of your equipment, you risk spending unnecessarily elsewhere in hidden costs – energy, labour and maintenance.

Expert Opinion: Archstone Consulting

Storage hardware provides a good example. Data storage is an area of explosive growth for many data centre, tempting many CIOs to ignore their refresh policies and keep operating existing storage hardware for as long as possible. However, operating costs for storage hardware can sharply increase over time. Many storage vendors drastically increase the price of hardware maintenance in the fourth and fifth years of ownership and new units can be significantly more power efficient on a raw per-gigabyte basis. A properly constructed hardware refresh policy will guide you to make the right trade-offs between conserving capital and missing out on lower maintenance and power costs.

There is also a danger inherent to being too strict in your refresh cycle. If you set a strict timeframe that dictates all servers are upgraded every three years, for example, you may be tossing out equipment still more than capable of delivering an extra year or two of service. You may even replace equipment only to find later that it was being phased out anyway.

The rate at which hardware should be refreshed varies from item to item and company to company depending on use, need and a myriad of other factors. There is no 'one size fits all' timetable that you can adhere to. When determining your own hardware refresh and upgrade lifecycle you'll need to invest time and consideration in finding the sweet spot; the trade off between expenditure and operational efficiency.

The most helpful way to create a useful refresh policy is to proceed on an applic ation-by-application basis. For each one, consider not just the item's age but its past, present and predicted future usage statistics.

Archstone Consulting suggests a five technology towers approach:

1. Server
2. Storage
3. Network
4. Workstation
5. Security

Each tower should then be split into its relevant sub-categories.

The subsequent refresh policy should then consider:

- What is required of this application?

- What roadmaps are associated with this application?

- What are the capacity planning and utilization targets?

- Do opportunities exist to consolidate cycles?

- Is there the option to upgrade hardware components?

- Are dramatic technology changes on the horizon? What developments are just around the corner?

- What is the pricing system?

- How reliable is this application? What are its performance statistics?

What are the Benefits of Creating a Refresh Policy?

The payoffs for investing time and resources in creating a refresh policy rather than dealing with breakages and break downs ad-hoc as they arise are both multiple and scalable. If you get it right, your refresh policy will be advantageous from both an operational and financial perspective, which is what makes it such an intrinsic part of our hardware and software activity.

From a purely practical and operational viewpoint, a refresh cycle will dramatically reduce the risk of component failure. This means no unexpected system crashes, no wasted downtime (or a minimised downtime in the event of a problem) and a reduced risk of incident. The addition of new or upgraded hardware at relevant points should also deliver operational opportunities, be they for increased capacity, productivity or production. Systems also become more secure as hardware that is no longer secure or supported is phased out at appropriate intervals.

From a balance sheet perspective, your refresh cycle should reduce capital expense and operating expense. It should address how the IT budget can be made more transparent and more accountable and make financial planning for future needs much easier. There is also the possibility to centralize funding and plan needed access to finance to coincide with product lifecycles. **Source of image:** http://www.wdpi.com/hardware-lifecycle-management

VINROSE NALUYANGE

2

WEB PRESENCE AND PORTALS

A web presence is fundamental to success in today's increasingly digitized business environment. It is an essential and core part of your business infrastructure and as such, requires a dedicated focus and generous allocation of resources. It drives sales and brand image, acts as a marketing function, can carry out customer service functions and in the case of an ecommerce site can also manage stock control, invoicing and order processing behind the scenes.

A web presence should not be considered as something static. It is fluid and dynamic and should be changed and updated often. While your core website may remain the same, certain parts of it should be updated frequently, making a suitable content management system or blog platform a necessary consideration.

When embarking upon the complex task of developing a web presence, various skill sets, hardware, software and technologies are required. You have a range of choices when it comes to programming languages but are advised to stick to something basic such as HTML rather than the more complicated Flash which will require more dedicated technologies and raises compatibility issues for the end user.

You'll need to select a suitable hosting and server and consider if you need a My SQL database so that the site is parked safely in cyberspace. You may need an additional bolt on to verify your safe neighbourhood such as a secure server certificate (SSL), which is essential if you want to process payments online via a provider such as WorldPay.

To process payments online you'll need a virtual terminal and a merchant account. You'll also need a virtual invoicing system, so you'll have to either link your CRM to the site or more commonly, opt for a content management system (CMS) or business application that can perform this function. If you don't want to or are unable to set up a merchant account, solutions such as PayPal can be easily integrated and don't require any additional resources such as processing in order to run successfully.

3

CYBER CRIME

Cyber crime is big business. In June 2013, the latest available figures estimated that cyber crime and cyber spying cost the global economy as much as $300 billion per year. The US loses out to the tune of around $100 billion per year, making cyber crimes more lucrative than the drug trade. But what is it, how is it perpetrated and what safeguards do you need to put in place to protect your systems and your organisation?

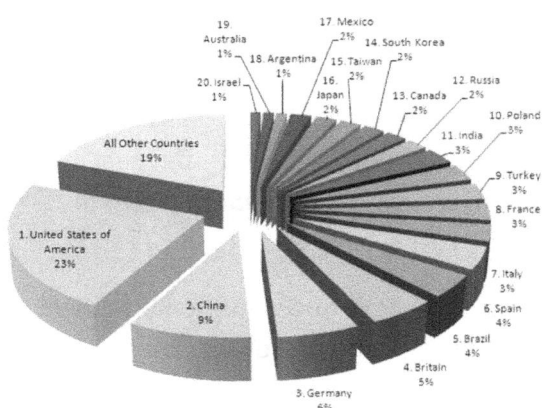

Cybercrime: Top 20 Countries

The Enterprise Strategy Group research study of 315 North American IT Security professionals confirmed that incidents of cyber security attacks have notably increased in the last two years.

Cyber attacks are not only more frequent, they are more sophisticated and more targeted. Many of those surveys said that endpoint security software is not effective at detecting evolving threats, such as those launched on systems by zero-day malware and Trojans.

The study found that:

- 29 per cent of respondent organizations that have suffered a successful malware attack believe the increasing use of social networks is responsible for those attacks

- On average, it takes 57 per cent of respondents' a significant number of hours to detect a that an IT asset has been compromised by malware and 19 percent can take days

- 74 per cent of enterprises have increased their security budget over the past 24 months in direct response to more sophisticated malware threats

- 62 per cent of respondents believe their host-based security software is not effective for detecting zero day and/or polymorphic threats

- 85 per cent of IT security professionals, given everything they know about cyber security, are concerned about some type of massive cyber-attack that could impact critical infrastructure, the economy, and/or national security

- 66 per cent of US.-based respondents do not believe the U.S. Federal Government is doing enough to help the private sector cope with the current cyber security and threat landscape.

The cost of cyber crime absorbed by small business is around £785 million per year (source: <u>Federation of Small Businesses, Cyber security and fraud: the impact on small businesses</u> report). Many small businesses are easy pickings because limited budgets mean they simply do not have the resources available to invest in high-end hardware and software systems to protect against online attacks.

However, there are simple steps that most small businesses can take to reduce their vulnerability to cyber crime and ensure that IT systems are not compromised. Companies that do not invest in appropriate security systems risk compromised IT infrastructures in which proprietary research, service or product information and even business control systems fall into the wrong hands. If your business is connected to the Internet, or if employees access the Internet using a business system, cyber security systems are an essential purchase.

Expert Opinion: Connectivity and Cyber Crime

In 2011, at least 2.3 billion people, the equivalent of more than one third of the world's total population, had access to the internet. Over 60 per cent of all internet users are in developing countries, with 45 per cent of all internet users below the age of 25 years. By the year 2017, it is

estimated that mobile broadband subscriptions will approach 70 per cent of the world's total population. By the year 2020, the number of networked devices (the 'internet of things') will outnumber people by six to one, transforming current conceptions of the internet. In the hyper connected world of tomorrow, it will become hard to imagine a 'computer crime', and perhaps any crime, that does not involve electronic evidence linked with internet protocol (IP) connectivity.

'Definitions' of cybercrime mostly depend upon the purpose of using the term. A limited number of acts against the confidentiality, integrity and availability of computer data or systems represent the core of cybercrime. Beyond this, however, computer-related acts for personal or financial gain or harm, including forms of identity-related crime, and computer content-related acts (all of which fall within a wider meaning of the term 'cybercrime') do not lend themselves easily to efforts to arrive at legal definitions of the aggregate term.

Certain definitions are required for the core of cybercrime acts. However, a 'definition' of cybercrime is not as relevant for other purposes, such as defining the scope of specialized investigative and international cooperation powers, which are better focused on electronic evidence for any crime, rather than a broad, artificial 'cybercrime' construct.

Extracted from Comprehensive Study on Cyber Crime, Draft – February 2013, United Nations Office on Drugs and Crime.

What Types of Cyber Threats is Your Network Most Likely to Come Up Against Online?

Network security threats can be structured or unstructured, internal or external. However you connect to the internet, whether you have a wired or Wi-Fi system, whether you log on all day long and conduct the majority of your business online or do nothing more than send a few emails, any network which is internet enabled is at risk from cyber crime and its associated threats.

Structured Threats: A Structured threat comes from a cyber criminal professional; a group, a single person or an organisation skilled in hacking and proficient at cyber crime. These structured threats can compromise your hardware and software and put your entire network at risk. Possible targets

include sensitive data such as product development information, staff records, price lists or company plans. They may commit fraud, change records or immobilise your network.

Types of Network Security Threats

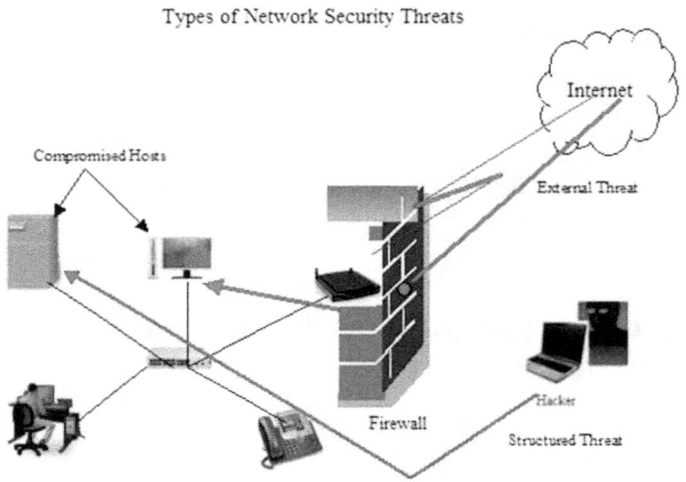

Source: http://www.orbit-computer-solutions.com/Threats-to-Physical-and-Network-Infrastructure.php

Unstructured threats: An unstructured threat comes from someone who is not a professional hacker but these less experienced attacks should still be feared. The methods used to squirrel into your network will be less sophisticated but once there, they can still wreak havoc.

A password cracker that gets a non-authorised person into your website can lead to your web presence being compromised – there have been

a number of instances of activists hacking into websites and changing text or displaying their own message on your company page.

There are multiple examples of celebrities and high profile businesses finding their social media accounts such as Facebook or Twitter have been hacked, with embarrassing messages posted for fans to see.

Internal Threats: An internal threat is one that looms large for many organisations, occurring when someone from inside your business with authorised and legitimate access to a system uses it for illegitimate ends.

External Threats: An external threat is mainly conducted through the medium of the internet. A hacker or someone with no authorised access to your business systems uses the medium of the internet to gain access to your network and systems.

Taking Action against Cyber Crime

The British Government estimates that around 80% of all cyber attacks can be defeated when appropriate information security systems are embedded across people, processes and technology.

Before you can select and install relevant systems to protect your intellectual property, hardware and software systems, there are a number of questions to ask:

Where are cyber security threats concentrated and who are you protecting systems against? A growing band of cyber criminals have risen up to profit from information obtained illegally online. Competitors can also benefit from sensitive information. Hackers may interfere with systems simply because they can; even employees pose a threat through accidental or deliberate actions.

Where do threats come from? Technical threats such as malware, spyware, viruses and Trojans are not the only points of entry for cyber criminals. Social engineering is on the rise – with emails supposedly sent from known acquaintances containing malicious links, passwords unwittingly being disclosed or networks left open.

What value does your information have? Before you can decide on an appropriate method of protection, you must first assign value to the information stored on your IT systems. Client data, supplier databases, pricing structures, business proposals, employee information, processes and schedules, and even your website and marketing campaigns must all be prioritised according to their importance.

What information do you need to protect? A review of information assets will help you categorise according to which data is most critical to your business operations.

How much risk is acceptable? Quantifying an acceptable risk threshold may seem like an alien concept but it can help you when deciding on the level of cyber security system to invest in. When deciding how much risk is acceptable, consider the information assets you have already identified, who has access to them and then act accordingly. Communicate how much risk is acceptable to those with authorised access to ensure that systems operate at the correct security level as standard; one employee having a mid range virus protection set is no use if someone else with the same access level has the anti-virus level on their machine set to low.

What measures are appropriate? Having identified risk appetite and defined which data needs the greatest levels of protection, you can now decide which security measures are needed to protect data from cyber criminality.

Some experts suggest that developing a basic information risk management strategy, coupled with appropriate end-zone security software reduces risk by up to 80%.

Expert Opinion: First Hand Experience

Excerpt from Computer Weekly article (http://www.computerweekly.com/news/2240083532/How-to-implement-role-based-access-control): A contractor had been working on a system within a company, and the firm discovered that he had been abusing his access rights.

"They discovered the guy was going in and doing things he had no business doing. He was pulling intellectual property out of the system and doing all kinds of horrid things," Enderle says.

Role-based access control is designed to prevent that situation arising. In most companies' systems, you will find different user accounts scattered throughout various applications in the organization. Those user accounts may have a few different levels offering different privileges, but they are unlikely to reflect the complex combinations of privileges present in the hierarchy of employee roles.

Not tying account privileges to real-world company roles leaves networks open to both external attack from hackers, who compromise user accounts, and internal attack from users abusing privileges that they should not have.

This vulnerability helped Robert Hanssen to deliver much valuable intelligence to the Soviets. Hanssen, an FBI agent, was arrested in 2001 for selling secrets to the Russians. Hanssen's arrest triggered a security review that found the FBI's network wanting. In the resulting congressional statement Hanssen said "any clerk at the Bureau" could have done what he did.

Five years on, the General Accounting Office delivered the results of another FBI network security review. It was still in grave danger of compromise.

What Types of Systems need to be in Place to Protect against Cyber Crime?

The security measures you put into place must be commensurate with the amount of risk you are prepared to tolerate in the face of cyber crime. In addition to selecting and installing appropriate security and anti-virus software, there are other systems and processes that you can put in place to ward off the threat of online crime.

1. **A mobile working policy**: If your staff work remotely either full time, part time or occasionally, for example when out at a meeting with clients, draft a mobile work policy. Provide copies of the policy to all staff and ensure that they both understand and implement it as a matter of course. Apply a secure baseline build to all mobile devices, whether they are smartphones, tablets such as an iPad or even laptops. Your data is then enshrouded in a layer of protection while on the move and outside of the office when connected to the internet via non-fixed means including BYOD.

2. **Assign user privileges and access levels**: Not all employees need the same level of access to data, networks and systems. A customer service rep does not need access to your sales intranet for example. Establishing accounts of varying access levels and restricting the number of accounts with full privileged access

can help to keep your systems secure. Your marketing team's junior assistant, for example, may need access to the company news page on the website in order to upload press releases, but they will not need access to all of the other website pages which lie outside of their area of responsibility.

Control access to systems and maintain activity logs to ensure that privileges are being used appropriately and passwords and access levels are not shared.

3. **Security configuration**: Implement a strict ICT secure configuration policy and apply appropriate security patches across your network.

4. **Install malware protection**: Malware is software that sits online and attempts to damage your computer or infect your website. You can apply malware protection across your network. You should regularly scan for malware and ensure your chosen malware protection is up-to-date to protect against new threats. Do not download your malware protection from the internet as this could already be infected.

5. **Create a control strategy for removable media**: If you have any removable media devices in your organisation, ensure that you have a sufficient, robust control strategy in

place to maintain their integrity. Ensure access to removable media is controlled and that all devices are scanned for malware and other threats before they are used on your systems.

6. **Maintain clear, focused network security**: Networks must be protected against both internal and external threats. Implementing firewalls and intrusion detection software is a good place to start; but it is worth investigating other ways you can maintain the integrity of the network perimeter as your first line of defence against cyber criminals. Regular monitoring and testing of security controls is essential, as is an ability to filter out unauthorised access. An anti-virus system should be in place to scan thee pages and prevent access to malicious content (online pages that may have spyware or malware embedded within).

7. **Incident management:** A disaster recovery and business continuity plan is not just for natural disasters such as fire and floods. Ensure that you also have a management policy in place for online incidents so that downtime is minimised and capability recovered as soon as possible.

Source: http://www.saleschase.com/blog/technology/

4

DIGITAL FORENSICS

Digital forensics is a relatively new discipline, emerging in the 1970s when personal computers first started to gain in popularity. It is an offshoot of the traditional forensics discipline and was originally established as computer forensics, before changing and adapting to take into account the myriad of digital devices capable of storing data and transporting it.

There are a number of instances in which you may need to call upon the discipline of digital forensics though it is most likely you'll need this service as part of investigations into an authorized network intrusion. If your systems have been breached and network put at risk, employing digital forensics tactics will shed light on how the breach occurred and the extent of the problem. It may also be used as a prelude to criminal proceedings.

Technically, digital forensics, much like its non digital and traditional counterpart is exceptionally complicated with various disciplines and sub-disciplines. The many disciplines or branches of digital forensics are typically split into categories which are themselves based on the device involved. These include:

Computer Forensics

Also referred to as computer science, computer forensics emerged in response to growing computer crimes such as hacking. Computer forensics was developed as a means of recovering and then investigating digital evidence; i.e., that found in computer systems, storage devices and electronic documents such as pictures or emails. Computer forensics can be used to retrieve information or to reconstruct a series of events and have been admissible in criminal law cases since the 1980s.

Famous examples of computer forensics being used in court include the case of Dennis Radar, a serial killer who sent police letters on a floppy disk. Computer forensics recovered meta-data from the device which led to his arrest. A more recent example is that of Dr. Conrad Murray, the physician whose conviction in the death of pop singer, Michael Jackson, was made possible by documents discovered on his computer relating to prescription amounts.

Network Forensics

Network forensics relates specifically to monitoring and analyzing network traffic. This is often needed to gather legal evidence if a crime has been committed, to gather information if a crime or failing is suspected and to detect intrusions in the case of a security breach or even a pre-emptive security sweep.

Because of the nature of network traffic, network forensics relate to dynamic information that is transmitted and then lost. This means that network forensics are pro-active – you may want to employ a network forensic expert to monitor your network traffic for suspicious activity or possible threats.

When a crime has been committed or suspected, a network forensics team can be called in to analyse recorded network traffic to complete important tasks such as reassembling files that were transferred on the network or parsing emails and chat sessions.

Network forensics are only possible if you have a strong security system in place which includes network firewalls, packet filters and intrusion detection systems.

Forensic Data Analysis (FDA)

Forensic Data Analysis (FDA) relates to the examination of structured data when financial crimes have occurred. The aim of FDA and its primary purpose is to discover and then analyse any data patterns which can prove a crime has been committed. FDA uses data which is pulled from databases in the system or from system applications using keywords or by mapping patterns in communications. The analysis will typically focus on the data itself rather than on the system or database that housed it.

Mobile Device Forensics

Mobile phones, tablets and other mobile devices are increasingly as essential as standard hardware and software systems to the modern business. Along with the boom in this type of equipment has come mobile device forensics, which has been developed to recover data from these types of devices. It is still a new and developing area of digital forensics, having emerged around the year 2000.

Mobile devices are incredibly useful business systems and many organisations would struggle to be as effective and efficient as they are without some form of mobile inventory for employees. However, along with this advent of new technology and new working methods comes new data such as SMS and MMS messages. Smartphones and tablets also contain other data such as web browsing histories and multimedia content in the form of videos and images as well as documents such as written text and data in spreadsheets.

Conducting a Digital Forensics Investigation

Because the field of forensics is such a specialist one, it is strongly recommended that you call in a dedicated forensics team should you need to run an investigation on your systems or network. This will help to ensure legal requirements for the data (authenticity and integrity) are maintained so that the information can be used if criminal proceedings are undertaken. A digital forensics team will generally conduct the investigation in three distinct stages:

1. **Acquisition of exhibits**: This may be done by making a duplicate of your system or if you use applications such as cloud computing or similar, accessing the live version.

2. **Analysis of data**: A full data analysis will determine whether or not a breach or crime has been committed and the extent of the problem. The International Journal of Digital Evidence defines this part of the process as "an in-depth systematic search of evidence related to the suspected crime".

3. **Reporting of findings**: A complete overview of what has been found and what that means.

5

GREEN COMPUTING

Green computing goes under a number of guises and the way that you identify it will depend on your organisation's culture. It may be referred to simply as green computing, as green IT, as green technology or as ICT Sustainability.

In essence, developing a green computing policy is a stated commitment to using computers and their associated hardware and software resources in an environmentally responsible or more eco-friendly manner.

Green computing in practise can involve a range of applications and business processes, from investing in more energy efficient CPUs when your hardware is ready for upgrade, to opting for cloud computing instead of traditional data centre storage facilities. It also covers reducing resources such as printed documents and the development of a suitable e-waste disposal policy.

Why Is Green Computing Important?

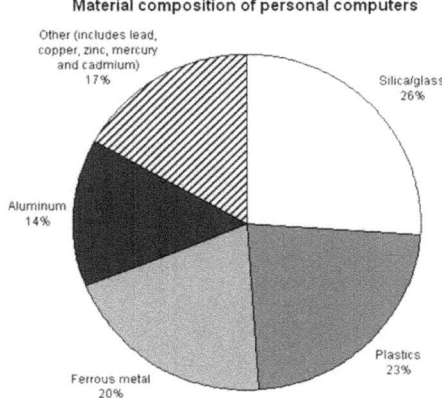

Material composition of personal computers

Other (includes lead, copper, zinc, mercury and cadmium) 17%

Silica/glass 26%

Aluminum 14%

Plastics 23%

Ferrous metal 20%

Source: Environment Canada.

The United Nations estimates that it takes as much as 1.8 tons of chemicals, fossil fuels and water to produce a typical desktop computer.

In 2010, Greenpeace reported that only two out of the biggest 18 computer and electronics manufacturers were actually producing reasonably energy friendly computers.

A 2009 report by Harris Interactive, commissioned by E Ltd and the Alliance to Save Energy, found that $2.8 billion a year was wasted just by US office workers not turning off their PCs at the end of the working day.

Intel estimates that as much as 60% of energy is wasted by non aggressive power management of business computers.

For many companies, corporate social responsibility is increasingly important. A CSR policy is a company-wide commitment which can win favour with clients, stakeholders and shareholders. Green computing is often central to these goals as it is a main driver in reducing wasted energy consumption, meeting recycling targets and operating as a more socially and environmentally responsible business.

Green computing is not just another IT buzz word. It is an important way to reduce the carbon footprint, cut down on CO_2 emissions and make significant energy savings, which deliver tangible cost benefits.

In June 2013, the prestigious American University Berkley encapsulated this potential very clearly with a study funded by Google. They discovered that moving just three common software applications from local computer systems to a centralized cloud service cut IT energy consumption by as much as 87% or 23 billion kilowatt-hours. The report estimates that this one saving is equivalent to the total amount of electricity used in a whole year by every business, home and industry in the city of Los Angeles.

Eric Masanet, lead author of the report warns, *"We can't fly by the seat of our pants when it comes to assessing sustainability. We need numbers – hard data — to properly analyze how cloud computing compares to how computing is done now. Well-thought-out analysis is especially important with new technology, which can have unforeseen effects. Our public model allows us to look forward and make informed decisions. What we found overall is that by hosting services on the cloud as opposed to locally, the savings are pretty robust."*

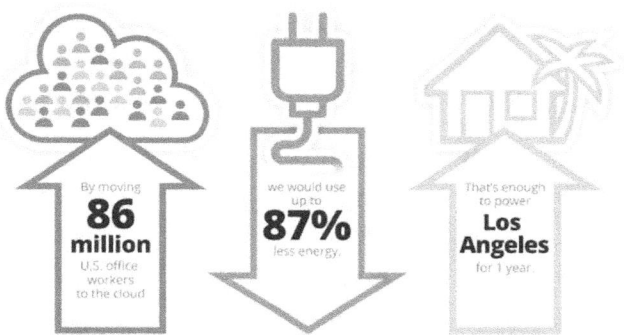

Source: http://newscenter.lbl.gov/news-releases /2013 /06/11/berkeley-lab-study-finds-moving-select-computer-services-to-the-cloud-promises-significant-energy-savings/

How Can Computing Go Green?

There are a number of ways your company can make wise choices in relation to its hardware and software setup and resources. Green computing has its roots in both strands, with savings to be made by making savvy choices when it comes to applications such as CRM systems as well as hardware models such as CPUs.

Implementing a green computing strategy can be undertaken at any stage of your purchase, refresh and upgrade lifecycle. You can favour more energy-saving hardware when purchasing a new item, which is of course the best way to proceed, but there are also steps you can take to make existing components work greener, even if they are not as efficient by design as they could be.

Common applications can also be streamlined for significant savings by adopting new technologies such as cloud computing, which is an important consideration for all businesses who want to make their computing processes, systems and components more sustainable.

One example of how easy changes can be made is simply by implementing a company-wide mandate that requires all employees to turn each PC off at the power outlet each evening. Even if you shut down your computer system each evening, it still consumes energy if it is plugged into a live power outlet as this current keeps the motherboard partially powered. It remains in a partial power state while it waits for the current to reach full power – that is to say when you arrive back at work the next morning and press the power button on the tower to initiate the system for the day's work.

Shut down but not flicked off at the power outlet, a computer will use around 8W of electricity each hour. Overnight, over the weekend and throughout the year, this consumption racks up, particularly if you have dozens of machines running in this way.

So how do you go about drawing all of these possibilities together and making your computing greener? What measures need to be implemented? How should they be adopted?

Expert Opinion: TechTarget Search Data Centre

The work habits of computer users and businesses can be modified to minimize adverse impact on the global environment. Here are some steps that can be taken:

- Power-down the CPU and all peripherals during extended periods of inactivity.

- Try to do computer-related tasks during contiguous, intensive blocks of time, leaving hardware off at other times.

- Power-up and power-down energy-intensive peripherals such as laser printers according to need.

- Use liquid-crystal-display (LCD) monitors rather than cathode-ray-tube (CRT) monitors.

- Use notebook computers rather than desktop computers whenever possible.

- Use the power-management features to turn off hard drives and displays after several minutes of inactivity.

- Minimize the use of paper and properly recycle waste paper.

- Dispose of e-waste according to federal, state and local regulations.

- Employ alternative energy sources for computing workstations, servers, networks and data centres.

Source: http://searchdatacenter.techtarget.com/definition/green-computing

Experts have put forward a suggested six areas in which small- and medium-sized businesses can make fundamental changes to their software and hardware processes in order to become greener.

As you set about considering the benefits and impact of green computing and begin to develop a green computing policy that overarches your selection and use of hardware and software systems, this six-point framework will provide a useful starting point. It is worth grouping your intended measures under these categories and using each heading to help you construct a new greener IT methodology.

Local Power Hardware

The greener hardware movement was sparked by Intel in 2005 when it unveiled a brand new concept – rather than focus on processor speed, it was recasting its net to incorporate hardware performance based on wattage. This means using lower-powered processors such as their Atom processor, which work more efficiently, incorporated rather than separate graphics cards; new passive cooling systems rather than traditional fans, and the use of solid state drives (SSD) in place of the older style of spinning disk storage.

The Intel work done on the Atom processor has led to a whole new generation of hardware options including lower wattage PCs and low energy hard disks, which can give up to 40% power consumption saving.

Before investing in a low power PC you will need to consider your system needs. Do you need to edit videos or operate a large number of multimedia files? If so, many of the lower powered PCs won't be suitable, as their power savings come at the cost of some functionality. However, this is changing all the time and there are other more energy-friendly measures you can adopt in the meantime.

Virtualization

Virtualization is typically centred on data centres, which consume a lot of power and are responsible for both excess energy usage and carbon emissions.

The US department for Energy Efficiency and Renewable Energy estimates that a typical data centre achieves only 15% energy efficiency which means 85% of energy is wasted.

In America alone, data centres use around $4.5 billion of electricity annually, according to an Energy Star study (see Infographic).

Data Center Energy Efficiency = 15% (or less)

(Energy Efficiency = Useful computation / Total Source Energy)

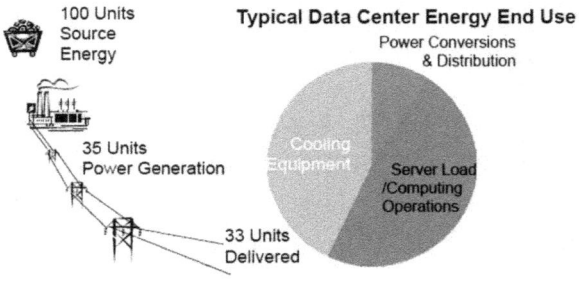

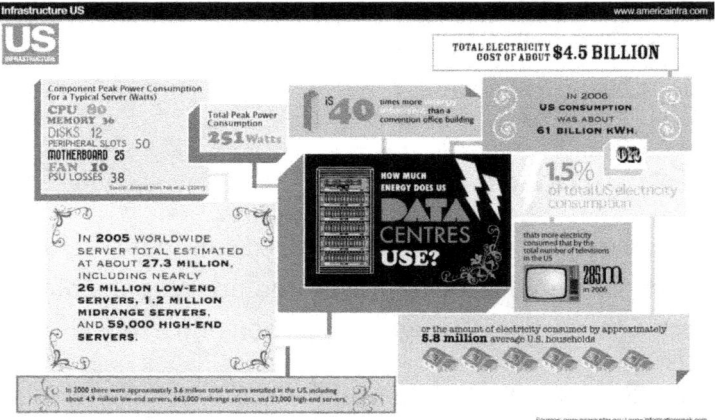

If you opt for virtualization, you take a very big step towards reducing your energy consumption, making it of considerable interest if you make use of a data centre.

Although it sounds like a complicated prospect, virtualization can be explained simply as the use of software rather than hardware. In a data centre scenario, rather than purchasing a physical server, you would use a virtual server software tool running on multiple machines. This emulates the function of server hardware but is encased within a software program. This method of arranging a data centre is very efficient because computing resources are optimised and also, wasted or idle server capacity is diminished.

Virtualization can also be carried out at file level which splits the storage of often accessed and infrequently accessed files across a range of drives.

A virtual rather than physical server leads to savings in energy and cooling costs.

6

CLOUD COMPUTING

Cloud computing is intrinsically linked to green computing and is a way of any business, whether large or small, to make its software applications greener with little required in the way of initial investment. It gives the benefits of virtualisation and is a proven way to reduce your firm's carbon footprint. Cloud computing is also linked to greener hardware as this can harness the power of SaaS in the cloud to

make powerful and more costly computer hardware unnecessary. This topic is covered in more detail later in this chapter.

Energy Efficient Coding

For those serious about going green, choosing software applications which boost energy efficient coding credentials is advisable. Energy efficient coding means that the software is written in such a way that it places less of a burden on the hardware, allowing for less power usage.

Recycling of Electronic Waste

What is e-waste?

Breakdown of electronic and electrical waste in the European Union

Electrical: 50% of total

30%
Washing machines, dryers, air conditioners, vacuum cleaners, coffee machines, toasters, irons etc

20%
Refrigerators

Electronic: 50% of total

15%
DVD/VCR players, CD players, radios, Hi-Fi sets etc.

15%
Computers, telephones, fax, printers etc

10%
Televisions

10%
Monitors

Source: EMPA Swiss Federal Laboratories for Materials Testing & Research

A growing issue

E-waste generated worldwide in 2009

53 million tonnes

13% was recycled

Source: ABI Research

Mobile phone subscriptions per 100 inhabitants, EU 27

1997: 12, 1998: 20, 1999: 33, 2000: 53, 2001: 65, 2002: 71, 2003: 78, 2004: 87, 2005: 96, 2006: 106, 2007: 116, 2008: 122

Source: Eurostat

Why e-waste is a problem

Electronic waste is valuable but can be hazardous

An average mobile phone contains more than 45 elements including

Lead (Pb), Antimony (Sb), Arsenic (As), Beryllium (Be)

Platinum (Pt), Palladium (Pd), Silver (Ag), Gold (Au), Copper (Cu)

Cobalt (Co)

(Li-Ion battery)

Valuable   Toxic

Source: Umicore

Recycling is of course the poster child of being more energy efficient, and while many will be familiar with programs to recycle and reuse plastic, paper and glass, electronic waste recycling has lagged behind. Electronic waste takes many forms with around 15% estimated to be from computers and 10% from monitors.

The World's electronic waste streams are unevenly distributed and many nations and governments are beginning to tackle this problem by creating e-waste directives and targets. As a business, it is possible to take more responsibility for how unwanted electronic items, such as computer monitors and other hardware, are disposed of. This can have financial as well as environmental benefits. Your electronic waste strategy may incorporate such actions as recycling internal components from computers that are being retired into other machines, or perhaps keeping them as spares in the event of a system breakdown. They can also be sold on to a firm that specialised in e-waste recycling and refurbishment or donated to worthy causes.

Other Ways to Take Your Computing Green

There are also other ways in which you can introduce green computing to the very fabric of your organisation's culture. Not only in terms of the hardware you buy and the power you use but in making use of new applications such as mobile working to reduce the number of miles employees travel or commute to the office.

Video conferencing can replace the need to travel to client meetings and can mean that costly airline tickets are a thing of the past. A report by the European Telecommunications Network Operators Association calculates that video conferencing alone could save 22.35 million tons of carbon dioxide a year by reducing travel.

The same report also estimates that if all EU states introduced online billing for services such as mobile phones, a massive 686 million tons of emissions would be saved annually. You can put this practise to work by implementing virtual billing and considering online invoicing applications in place of traditional print and paper.

You can invest in SaaS (Software as a Service) practices rather than purchasing software and hardware, therefore reducing spend and lowering your carbon footprint.

Cloud Computing

Cloud computing is a term coined fairly recently to describe the way that businesses large and small can use files and applications that are stored online rather than on a local system. Infoworld describes the cloud as,

"...A way to increase capacity or add capabilities on the fly without investing in new infrastructure, training new personnel, or licensing new software. Cloud computing encompasses any subscription-based or pay-per-use service that, in real time over the Internet, extends ITs existing capabilities."

The cloud has a number of benefits for small- to medium-sized businesses because it makes a series of practices possible and realistic – cost and efficiency measures such as remote working, real time access to data streams and access to company data from any device; whether in the office, on site, at work, at home or whilst commuting. Some studies suggest that using cloud computing systems leads to a revenue growth, while others confirm that it is more efficient from an energy and green perspective.

Adopting a cloud computing methodology is often seen as a way to drive forwards an innovating mindset, particularly for smaller businesses, for which the cloud is often a leveller playing field when going up against the resources and technology of much larger competitors.

Using the cloud to implement SaaS solutions can be used to create value, both by reducing spend in physical solutions and in facilitating more energy efficient working processes.

Using the cloud has additional security benefits: whereas CIOs would previously struggle to monitor access from multiple devices in many locations, the cloud provides a single access point and control centre. Entire business models can be run from the cloud, making growth easier as new users can simply be given access to systems as needed, regardless of whether they are sat at a desk in your office or sitting at their own desk halfway around the world.

Speaking to The Guardian, cloud computing expert Simon Withers, the vice president of Global Cloud Products at SunGuard Availability Systems said, "Ultimately, cloud has come so far that you can now run entire business processes on a resilient platform that offers unprecedented levels of availability for your enterprise, at a fraction of the previous price."

As a small business the potential to make huge strides forward is centred in the cloud, but uptake has been slow in some areas.

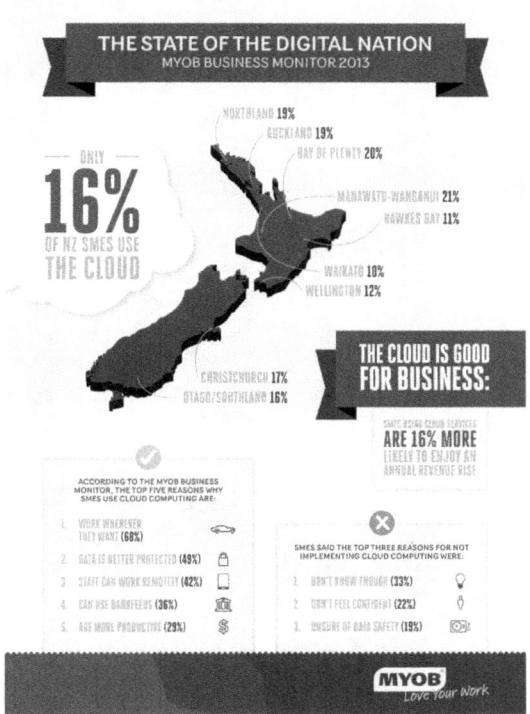

Source: http://myob.co.nz/blog/smes-missing-out-on-growth-opportunities/

Cloud Computing: SMBs' Secret Weapon

The move to the cloud represents a major opportunity for service providers, and partnering with Microsoft offers the most complete set of cloud-based solutions to meet SMB needs.

TODAY'S SMBs

They believe in themselves.

76% agree that SMBs are the backbone of the economy.

They are growing.

53% expect sales growth within the next 12-18 months.

They want to have more fun at work.

79% believe that technology can make work more enjoyable.

POTENTIAL FOR SUCCESS

They are increasingly moving to the cloud.

The number of very small companies (2-10 employees) using paid cloud services will triple in the next three years.

They are growing more comfortable with cloud services.

65% expect to be using cloud email services in the next 2-3 years.

They think the cloud is important.

50% agree that cloud computing is going to become more important for businesses such as theirs.

CLOUD CONCERNS

They see security as a priority.

70% want to know where their data is located.

30% want it kept in their country.

On-premise versus cloud

Only about 20% believe that data is less secure in the cloud than it is in their on-premise system.

Opportunities for service providers

60% don't have resources to implement new technologies and applications.

MULTIPLE SERVICES, ONE VENDOR

They want one source for services.

56% prefer a single source for their IT, and many want a mix of applications and infrastructure sources.

They plan to use more cloud services.

Current cloud users report purchasing an average of 4 services in the cloud now and expect to use 6 in the future.

They want to be more mobile.

71% require technology that enables their staff to work anywhere at any time.

Microsoft | Operator Channels

Source: Edge Strategies survey commissioned by Microsoft Corp., "SMB Business in the Cloud 2012" Feb. 8, 2012.

If you are one of the many SMEs that are still debating what you may get out of cloud computing, it is worth considering the multitude of benefits that await you:

How You Can Start Cloud Computing as an SME

By its very nature of joining together such a multitude of applications and services, cloud computing offers a number of easy entrance points for small- and medium-sized businesses.

The most common application is via an SaaS platform and these are increasingly main stream, with SaaS brought increasingly direct to the desktop from providers such as Google and Google Apps, which include email, document creation and storage. Because SaaS uses multi-tenant architecture delivered to multiple clients, as an SME you can benefit from the bulk buy mentality – the costs are supported by so many customers that it is a cheap way of accessing otherwise costly systems. There is no upfront investment in software licenses or expensive server equipment and hosting costs are reasonable. Possible applications include HR tools and CRM systems.

As an offshoot of cloud-based SaaS, you can also make use of web apps to perform everyday functions at a lower cost – payroll is one such example, which negates the need to retain a professional payroll service provider or purchase a payroll processing software package. Resource intensive apps can also be migrated to the cloud, with one such example being an SQL Server and Exchange server. If you have lots of users attempting to access any kind of system like this at the same time, a large strain is placed on your own infrastructure.

Moving to the cloud means the cloud itself does the hard work, freeing up your own assets and streamlining working practises.

Data storage and virtual servers can also be accessed via cloud computing, again making for significant cost savings compared with investing in traditional solutions. Virtual data centres hosted in the cloud give you the chance to scale up your storage architecture without the need for physical space or the purchase of physical hardware.

If your business requires a development environment in order to conduct its activities, the cloud can also be pressed into service as a platform environment. This means you can build apps in the cloud and deliver to clients virtually via the internet. Although larger, both Adobe and Microsoft 365 have shown that this is a practical transition.

If you need a managed service provider to carry out a simple task such as scanning incoming emails for malicious attachments, viruses or other threats, the cloud can help.

7

MOBILE COMPUTING SECURITY

A survey by the Symantec Corporation in February 2012 concluded that mobile computing is at a tipping point, with at least 71 percent of enterprises at least discussing the use of mobile applications and one-third having already implemented them.

Introducing any type of mobile computing mechanism to your business has well-documented advantages (increased flexibility and productivity being just two). But along with this transportability comes inherent risks. With smartphones, laptops, tablets and mobile storage devices such as flash drives also susceptible to being lost, hacked or stolen, the data contained within them is also at risk, be it of a personal nature (phone numbers or SMS messages on the smartphone memory for example) or corporate (presentations for an upcoming meeting saved on an iPad for instance). Almost 50% of those surveyed by Symantec feel that mobile computing represents a security risk:

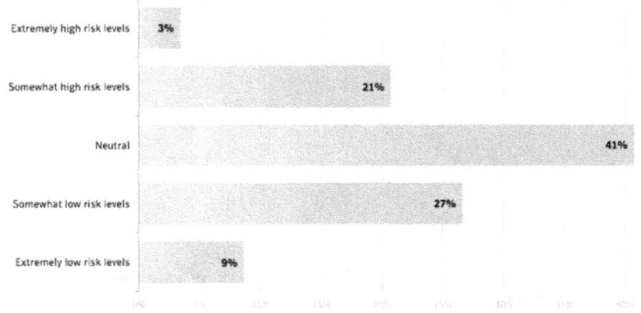

How would you characterize the level of risk your organization faces in conjunction with mobile computing?

- Extremely high risk levels — 3%
- Somewhat high risk levels — 21%
- Neutral — 41%
- Somewhat low risk levels — 27%
- Extremely low risk levels — 9%

Source: http://velositor.com/2012/04/11/almost-50-of-the-organizations-in-a-global-survey-feel-mobile-computing-is-somewhat-low-highly-risky/

Because they are designed to be taken from one place to another, mobile computing devices are at risk of being lost or stolen. Whether they are snatched from a bag or left by mistake on an aeroplane, it is easy for someone exterior to your organisation to access that material. Even if the tablet or smartphone remains in the hands of its rightful owner, mobile functionality such as Wi-Fi means that data can still be accessed unlawfully if the appropriate security measures and locks are not implemented. However, this is not to say that these issues are insurmountable.

An easy way to get started with a more secure mobile computing strategy is to create a list of prohibited and approved data. Set out what can and can't be stored on a mobile device. Areas you may want to consider excluding can include company banking details, client lists, client contact information and employee social security numbers.

A mobile security plan should also address not just what is stored, but on which device the information is stored. Excluding smartphones that have been jailbroken or unlocked is an obvious starting point. Similarly mobile devices that do not give a password function should also be excluded. Conversely, if a smartphone, tablet or laptop permits user accounts and password protection, activating the function will prohibit unlawful access should be device be lost or stolen.

Being vigilant about keeping all apps and operating systems up to date is also crucial; as this ensures that manufacturer approved security is maintained. Apps that are not updated will often develop security holes over time, giving easy access for unauthorised users, malware and viruses.

Where manufacturer offered tools such as the FindMyiPhone security app are offered, ensure they are set up. This can help to locate lost devices, minimising security risks.

BUSINESS
APPLICATIONS

INTRODUCTION

In this chapter, we will examine the business applications that the SME needs, how they should be chosen, what their advantages are and how they can be utilised effectively.

We will first explore the most common business applications, those tools systems and functions that are common to many small and medium sized businesses, regardless of their sector, size and geographic location. This will include familiar concepts such as ERP, CRM, BI.

Next, we'll look at whether an off-the-shelf solution will suffice or whether it is best to get a bespoke application that is crafted specifically to suit the needs, wants and structure of your business.

We'll also investigate the inherent advantages and disadvantages of using genuine and non-genuine software; whether savings can be made, and what factors to take into account before this decision is made.

Business intelligence is something that many firms increasingly rely on, but in a burgeoning marketplace and with so much data to sift though, it can be hard to get started and to know which way to turn. We will look at this conundrum and make practical suggestions regarding how to access meaningful business intelligence in order to turn the findings into a clear and coherent strategy for future development.

With the world constantly connected, no business can survive without a working knowledge of digital and online marketing. We'll take a look at the basics, weed out common misconceptions and provide a roadmap for popular online marketing techniques, with reference to considerations such as social media management and search engine optimisation.

Finally, against this backdrop, this chapter will conclude with an examination of application upgrade considerations and best practices.

COMING UP:

- Common applications for business: ERP, CRM, BI

- Off-the-shelf or custom made?

- Advantages and disadvantages of using genuine and non-genuine software

- Business Intelligence

- Digital and Online marketing

- Application Upgrades: Considerations and Best Practices

1

COMMON APPLICATIONS FOR BUSINESS: ERP, CRM, BI

Running any business, small or large, in any sector and in any location requires a plethora of knowledge, resources, organization skills and the assistance of a range of applications. There are thousands if not millions of business applications on the marketplace, which solve common and not so common problems alike. The challenge for any owner, manager or CIO is to determine which of these applications will add value and within that select group, which are the best of breed offerings most likely to get the job done and done well.

Business applications are typically categorised according to the function that they perform, which makes it somewhat easier to make a start on deciding what is needed and what is superfluous. This landscape includes everything from business-to-business systems which connect partners and resellers, to front-end, back-end and server side solutions.

Increasingly, the most common applications are – at least in part – cloud based. They may include dedicated solutions for easier parts ordering, offer a customer support system, HR systems and even email clients.

Within this vast pool of business applications, a few common names stick out:

- ERP: Enterprise Resource Planning

- CRM: Customer Relationship Management

- BI: Business intelligence

Enterprise Resource Planning (ERP)

ERP is a form of business management software that is increasingly useful in a fragmented marketplace. Originally considered a large business tool, where ERP was deployed to provide dedicated customization, data analysis and focused upgrade and deployment teams, ERP is increasingly finding a home, albeit in a slightly different way, with SMEs. A new breed of ERP applications are springing up which are specifically designed and adapted to manage the smaller needs of smaller firms. One way in which an enterprise level ERP and a small business ERP differ is in the amount of data that can be handled and the complexity of dashboards presented to the user. Perhaps pandering to the fact the small- and medium-sized businesses often do not have large IT functions, a small business ERP will be somewhat more user-friendly, ensuring investment delivers real user benefits.

Sometimes known as a lightweight ERP, a small business version of this application is nevertheless very powerful and increasingly worth considering, especially if you're on the cusp of a growth period. A small business system will cover all of the major operational streams of your organisation under one roof, from operations and marketing to development and sales. It is worth searching out a lightweight ERP rather than attempting to get to grips with enterprise level resource planning program. Look for one labelled as an SaaS system. You can expect to find project management, financial planning, warehouse management, accounting and even business management under an ERP solution.

So what questions should you be asking and what considerations are the key points when purchasing an ERP system? The obvious starting point is to define your business requirements; what exactly do you need the ERP system to do? To ensure that your answer is accurate, it's worth first outlining your business processes and recording how they may change as your organisation grows.

Do you have any technical restrictions? Although small business ERP systems are primarily software solutions which are cloud based, if you do have particular technology restrictions, these will need to be addressed with the ERP provider.

What is your budget? You'll likely already have a realistic figure in mind but you'll need to be prepared to be flexible. In addition to any license costs, be aware that setup fees may also apply and some vendors will also ask for maintenance fees and implementation.

What is your time frame? Even an SaaS system will require a time frame in which it can be implemented. It is best to avoid peak periods, so identify when the peaks and troughs are in your sales cycle. You'll need to factor in time for testing and training, rather than just installing the application.

CRM: Customer Relationship Management

A CRM application is an invaluable addition and will deal with any and all interactions between your business and its customers. Whether you are business-to-business or business-to-consumer focused, a CRM can be put to work automating, organizing and syncing a range of important functions – sales (for both current and future clients), marketing (to both current and future clients), offering technical support (current clients) and even managing customer service.

Your customers are your lifeblood, thus making a CRM an extremely important purchase. At a customer service level, it makes managing and creating customer service requests less prone to human error and more organised, ensuring queries are immediately assigned to a relevant representative and that client's issues are resolved.

If you carry out any form of marketing, a CRM can be used to manage and track campaign performance across a number of channels, collecting data from email marketing and direct mail to present an organised and global view of resulting leads, sales and actions. At a sales level, popular systems such as Salesforce.com have been proven to increase productivity and sales efficiency. In June 2013, this was recognised by Enterprise Apps Today, which denoted empowering sales managers as one of the top five CRM trends to watch in 2013. When it comes to choosing a CRM system, your options are many and varied.

Even with a narrowed down list of providers, you'll need to consider a number of factors before making your choice. Does your CRM system need to be cloud-based? What is your budget (obviously this will play an important role in the decision-making process)? Do you need a CRM that has multi-lingual capabilities?

The Sage CRM Dashboard

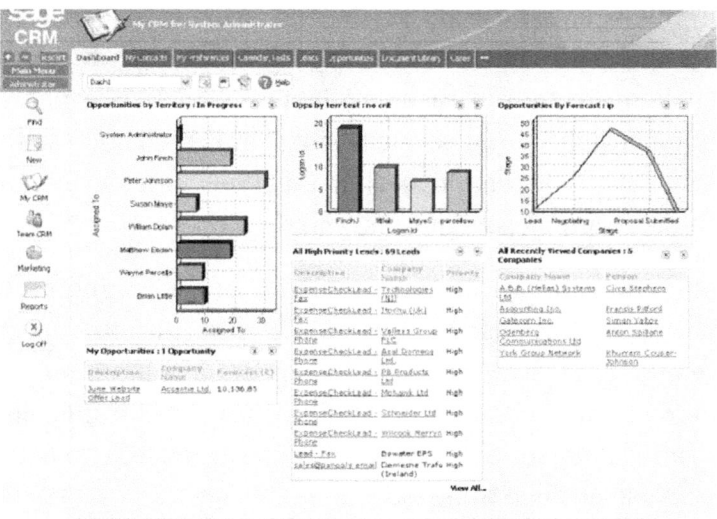

Source: http://www.armsoftware.com/sage-crm-integration

BI: Business Intelligence

If your business priorities include a move to cut costs, a desire to enhance the decision-making process or the need to be able to identify new business opportunities as they arise, a BI solution should be on your radar.

BI is rather a generic term as it actually refers to an entire collection of applications which come together to offer a number of complimentary functions, things like data processing, and analysis and reporting. If you are a business leader that tends to make decision based on instinct, a BI application can take the guesswork out of your actions by providing almost instant access to data and reports that can back up or show the fallacy in your intended plan of action.

One of the biggest challenges to using a BI system is in the rolling out process. Because BI is entirely based on the data that is input into the system, the first challenge comes in ensuring data is clean. BI is capable of incredibly complex calculations and can be met with scepticism by employees, making an extensive and robust training schedule essential.

Many businesses fall into the trap of dedicating long hours to the installation of the application but in reality, experts argue that as reports are intended to be dynamic and adapt to the business, it is a mistake to allocate resources tasked with creating ideal reports, because no such thing exists.

Finally, be sure that you really need a BI function. Some businesses can exist, and indeed thrive, without one. It is only a system that you can turn to if you know that number crunching will help to drive your objectives forward.

2

OFF THE SHELF OR CUSTOM MADE?

The build or buy conundrum is one that you are bound to face as you embark on a process of putting hardware and software systems in place. It is likely to be a question that you return to again and again throughout the course of your business activities, particularly as your organisation changes both in size and structure.

In some cases you'll find that you won't even have a choice as the apps that are available off-the-shelf will not meet all of your business needs. In other instances, you may have to decide if you want to compromise and use an app that meets 80% of your requirements or if the missing 20% is cause enough to build a bespoke solution.

This table, adapted from one developed by Bob Mango from 3C software, provides a helpful framework for the off the shelf or custom debate.

Building a Custom Solution

PROS	CONS
The system will meet your every need	Changes may be costly
The upfront cost may be lower	The entire project lifecycle from concept through to training is likely to be expensive
Fixes can be carried out immediately, as can enhancements	Resource availability may not be guaranteed
100% control over how much is spent to upgrade	No economy of scale for SMEs
May deliver a competitive advantage	Customizations can be challenging
Can be designed with legacy systems in mind	May be difficult to support new tech platforms as they emerge

Buying an off the shelf solution

PROS	CONS
The majority of your needs will be satisfied instantly	Any missing functionality is unlikely to be added
Quick deployment	The application isn't specific to your business
All design and development handled by the vender	You may need to take out a maintenance plan to access upgrades and enhancements
Choice of software licensing levels if you shop around	Enhancements may not be relevant to your business model
Knowledge base is established and spread over a number of resources	The upfront purchase costs may be high

3

ADVANTAGES AND DISADVANTAGES OF USING GENUINE AND NON-GENUINE SOFTWARE

The question of whether or not to use genuine or non-genuine software is as much an ethical one as it is a technical one. Non genuine software is usually pirated software which raises a heated debate when it comes to deciding if it's worth it.

Even if you're guilty of downloading music or films from file sharing sites, opting to use non-genuine software for your SME can have more serious implications than a guilty conscience.

Just as it is easy to access genuine software by walking into a shop or ordering online, sources of improperly licensed software are also many and varied. In the Harrison Group Whitepaper entitled Genuine Microsoft Products vs. Pirated Counterparts (August 26 2011), the software company Microsoft identified the following common sources of pirated software:

Transferred from another computer or borrowed from a friend: 7.2%

Downloaded from a peer-to-peer network or web site: 71.5%

Bought in a store, from a street market or from an online auction / supplier: 9.1%

Came with the computer: 12.2%

Genuine Vs. Pirated Software

When you purchase genuine software, you also invest in peace of mind. With a valid license you can be certain that all needed security upgrades and enhancements will be taken care of and that the quality of the security fixes is trustworthy. With non-genuine software there is no vender support, leaving your system open to security holes, intrusions and out-of-date protection that stems only from when the original copy was purchased.

As a business with data that you'll want to keep safe, a high price should be placed on the knowledge that software fixes and updates are genuine. With patches for non-genuine software, there is nothing to say that the update itself hasn't been infected with spyware, malware or a virus that puts your data and other systems at risk. In the Harrison Group white paper, research by Microsoft indicated that: *"24% of the machines running counterfeit software... either became infected at installation, or independently downloaded and installed malicious software upon connection to the internet"*.

When something goes wrong with a genuine app or software package, you benefit from vender or manufacturer assistance. When something unexpected goes wrong on a non-genuine copy, there is no-one to turn to in order to put things right and reduce downtime.

Buying a genuine copy also gives access to useful, complete and well-developed user instruction manuals, troubleshooting guides and how-to resources. Typically, these will be accessed at an account level, either online by logging in with a username and password or via telephone support. If you haven't purchased the software, you won't have an account with the vender, which means this helpful training framework is unavailable to staff members. Performance is also superior in genuine software compared with non genuine software. The Harrison report states that:

"In a recent study, IDC found that 36% of consumers had installed software on their machines that had slowed their computer so much that it had to be uninstalled, and 34% reported installing software that would not run at all*. Our study reinforces these findings, confirming that genuine Microsoft users tend to enjoy superior performance in the form of faster boot times, faster print times, faster document loading times, faster loading times when visiting popular text-and-graphics-heavy websites, and faster intranet page loading times than users of counterfeit products. The reduction in wait time for all of these common tasks adds up to a more dynamic, productive and satisfying experience for users of genuine Microsoft products."

In its summary of genuine vs. pirated software, the report concluded that:

Counterfeit users make significant sacrifices.

In total, our results indicate that counterfeit users pay a high cost for the low price of counterfeit software. Users of pirated software are opening themselves up to the potential for both catastrophic security breaches and significant losses in productivity and performance, regardless of the platform they use, and regardless of whether the counterfeit software's source is the web, a street market stall, or an unprincipled hardware retailer.

4

DIGITAL AND ONLINE MARKETING

Research from Reach Local suggests that a massive 97% of all customers will start the buying process online by researching potential suppliers before they make a purchase. This means that almost 100% of your sales are likely to begin life on the internet. If you are not employing digital and online marketing to its fullest, you are conceding a huge advantage to your competitors.

Having a web site is no longer a choice or a luxury, in a world that is switched on 24 hours a day, 7 days a week, it is a must. Once you have a website, online marketing is the means by which internet users can find it and by extension, your products and services.

From search engine optimisation (SEO) to pay per click (PPC) advertising, via AdWords, Facebook, Twitter, Pinterest, Google Hangouts, likes, tweets, pins, content marketing, email marketing, , blogging, banner ads, social media marketing, viral and YouTube, there are a million and one ways that you can get your name known online.

Where once online and digital conjured images of the black arts and were shrouded in mystery, the discipline has developed over the course of the last five or six years into a fusion of both art and science.

There are no quick fixes and competition is fierce. The landscape shifts frustratingly often and new technologies, buzzwords and platforms emerge and then recede at lightning speed. There is always a new hot technique, a new next big thing and invariably, a very crowded pool of so-called experts. Navigating all of this and sorting out what matters from what doesn't is time consuming; it can be disheartening and, unless you keep a very tight rein on the purse strings, expensive. It is undoubtedly a full time job.

Having said that the pitfalls are deep, it must also be said that the rewards are correspondingly high. No small business can afford to ignore online marketing because when it is done right, it connects your brand to your customer at the exact moment in which they are looking to purchase. It puts your business on an almost level playing field with the big guns and can be done entirely virtually – you don't even need an office to market yourself and your business and take orders virtually.

The way that you approach online marketing will very much depend on how much you have to spend. If you have the resources, it is worth allocating a part- or full-time member of staff to this marketing function as online success is not something that can be shoehorned into other parts of the day or business functions.

If you take a long term approach, search engine optimisation is the way to go. This is the process of optimising your website for certain key phrases to ensure that when a user types that word into Google, your website appears in the search results. The objective is of course to have your site appearing at number one. This does not happen overnight and the length of time will depend on the competition for each keyword (how many other pages are also listed for that same keyword).

There are hundreds if not thousands of software packages that claim to help you master SEO, but the reality is that it is an ongoing process. Do not fall into the trap of buying into hyperbole that promises to optimise your site and get you to number one. The search engines have very severe penalties in place for anyone attempting to game the system. The sensible approach is to carefully choose one or two useful software packages and then use those in conjunction with a skilled online marketeer.

Options include a rank tracker, which is a small piece of software that will monitor the position of your selected keywords on the main search engines. Page auditing software can point out where you're going wrong on each page of your website, generating useful data and reports that your real life online marketer can interpret.

Most online marketing requires very little specialist software. Social media marketing, for example, requires nothing more complex than an internet browser and someone who can create a social media page. There are apps available which will automate your social media updates for you and schedule posts, blogs, tweets and status updates which can be a real time saver.

The mantra that content is king has never been more relevant than it is today. And one way that you can use this to your advantage is to invest in a blog. You can download free blogging software from any number of sites but top apps to look out for include WordPress, TypePad and Blogger. A blog can be integrated into the back end of your website so your posts appear on your own domain or it can be hosted by the blogging platform. The choice is yours.

Although not directly related, one item that really is essential is a decent content management system. This is an application that drives all of the content on your website, allowing you to publish new content and add new pages. The rate at which you refresh your site and add new pages, along with the size of the site, is an important SEO factor. Without a CMS system, you'll need to hard code all changes, which is a time consuming way of maintaining a site.

Insist on a functional CMS system when your site is designed and you'll reap the benefits when it comes to online marketing. You can get a bespoke system designed, although these can be expensive; or opt for an off-the-shelf package such as the WordPress codex (which is free). CMS systems for e-commerce sites will also perform other functions, such as tracking stock and some will also process payments.

5

APPLICATION UPGRADES: CONSIDERATIONS AND BEST PRACTICES

When you have an application that is working well, is used appropriately by a well-trained employee base, and helps your business to run as well as it should, contemplating an upgrade can be a painful prospect.

"The most common reason that we hear for deferring an upgrade is the lack of a convincing business case. Sometimes, however, the perceived lack of benefits may be a result of incomplete analysis of the business process opportunities".

Forrester Research Inc. "Application Upgrades: How to Make Upgrade Decisions When Business Value Proves Elusive", June 2010

Deciding exactly when, how or why to upgrade business applications is a complex process. It can impact on a number of business areas, not least of which is operational capability. Indirectly, it can also have a knock-on effect on sales, customer service, marketing and finance functions.

The first question to ask when weighing up the case for making application upgrades is what the likely benefits are. A common consideration is whether or not the upgraded app will offer more security to your business. As apps become older, if not upgraded, the technology and coding that powers them becomes more susceptible to security breaches. So while the app may appear to be working as well as it always has, in the back ground it could be a ticking time bomb, just waiting to go off. When new versions of apps are released, it is always advisable to review the security updates and base a needs analysis on findings.

A second consideration is your own modernisation goals. If apps are rooted in outdated technology or linked to systems that are not as current as they could be, you need to ask if an upgrade will allow you to power forwards with modernisation needs.

Thirdly, a significant amount of attention needs to be paid to the end user experience. Although your employee base may be familiar with your current incarnation of apps and therefore feel that they are getting along with it quite well, an upgrade will often offer the chance to shake things up for the better.

As new versions of apps are released they tend to hone and refine the user experience. A need to increase operational output, reduce man power or improve efficiency, all make a strong case for considering a upgrade. New features, functions and new technologies may completely transform working processes, shaving valuable minutes off routine tasks or relieving staff from the burden of particular processes altogether – for example, by offering a report scheduling system where currently, reports have to be generated manually.

Compliance is often a cause for considering an upgrade; depending on the industry your business operates in and the regulatory burdens placed upon it, the decision as to when to upgrade may be taken out of your hands.

When the decision to upgrade has been made, best practise guidelines help to minimise disruption and smooth the path from old to new.

An initial audit is the first essential step on the road to best practise implementation. This process is a simple way of ensuring that the organisation has a true and accurate record of its application assets, as well as offering the all-important record of what is present in the production environment, which may well prove essential to application upgrade.

When the audit has been performed, the second stage of best practise is then to establish baselines. This is an important part of the upgrade process and is implemented to create initial standard installations of the application. Microsoft describes the baseline as, "... *the configuration of a product or system established at a specific point in time. An application or software baseline, for example, provides the ability to rebuild a computer to a specific state.*" (source: http://technet.microsoft.com/en-us/library/cc180701.aspx)

Ensuring that end users are included in best practice policy is also advisable, as this can help to prepare users for new applications as well as streamlining the transition process. Being aware of the end user when best practise is being created can also be critical to minimising downtime and disruption by effectively preparing them for new solutions and applications when they become available. Establishing awareness and training prior to deployment will help to minimize support issues when the new applications do go live.

PERFORMANCE AND SUPPORT

INTRODUCTION

In this section we will look at the challenges facing SMEs as they look to monitor performance, optimise performance and both offer and receive support.

Turning to staff training, we'll tackle the often thorny issue of how staff can best be brought up to speed, and how training can be delivered and aligned with company growth and service objectives.

We'll examine the software ecosystem, looking at what it is in accessible terms, how it works and what it can add to your business. Return on investment (ROI), which is such a critical business term, will also be examined in the context of performance, as well as the pros and cons of insourcing and outsourcing. If you're really not sure which way to turn, this particular section will provide clarity and thinking points to help your decision-making process.

Finally, we'll discuss customer support and how this essential business function can be nurtured, delivered and improved.

COMING UP:

❯ Staff Training

❯ Annual Maintenance Services

❯ Software Ecosystems

❯ Return on Investment

❯ Getting Support: Insourcing & Outsourcing

❯ Customer Support

1

STAFF TRAINING

SMEs face many problems and issues when it comes to the relevant staff training, mostly because of their size and the limited access they have to resources. Finding the capital to start a small business in the first place is a tough enough task, without setting enough money aside to send their team, however small, on a training course. It is a constant struggle to keep on top of quickly moving IT systems as well as the legislation they must conform to with regards to health and safety.

Human resources are said to be the key challenges to innovation plans for many businesses. But according to a survey in Europe, compiled by CEDEFOP, there are around 100 million workers across the continent who are at risk in their jobs due to their qualification levels, with around 20 million unemployed. 80 million people are considered low-skilled.

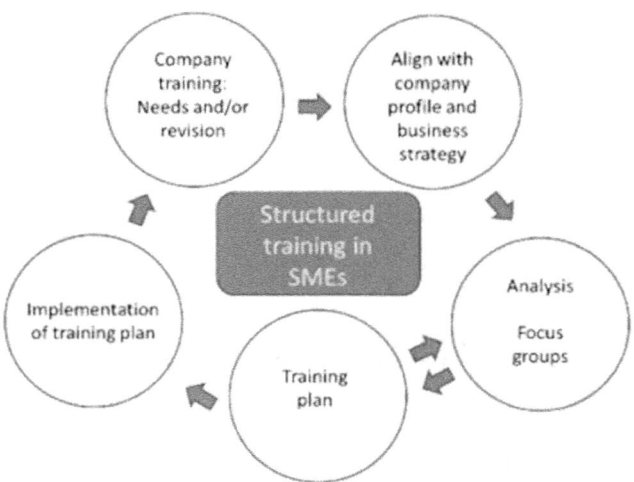

Source: http://t-planner.eu/

However, there is no hard and fast rule for all SMEs when it comes to training their staff and ensuring they are appropriately qualified. Each case must be treated with discretion; there is no single best solution for dealing with training issues, but there are frameworks which can be applied and answers which can address specific regions, industries, sectors and enterprises.

Before commencing training, it is important to establish which of the different training techniques will be used. E-learning and 'blended' learning are popular choices for those developing more general skills, and on-the-job training makes the most of a business's resources and means that staff members don't need to take time off to train. Traditional training sessions in a dedicated centre should not be overlooked; they are still highly effective, especially in areas such as manufacturing and construction where manual abilities will need to be demonstrated in detail.

There are a handful of keywords which can sum up the experiences of SMEs in the training sector.

Anticipation	In a rapidly changing economy, the anticipation of skills and competence should become second nature to SMEs. They need to be equipped with adapted tools and advice in human resource management.
Social Dialogue	Anticipating skills and competence implies plenty of dialogue between workers and employers. Assessment tools can offer an initial basis for this dialogue to be implemented. The proximity between managers/entrepreneurs and employees in small- and medium-sized companies provides many opportunities for a common construction of company plans with regard to human capital.
Assessment	A permanent, lifelong culture of assessment should be promoted. In the context of a knowledge society, skill needs are rapidly changing. Needs assessment is therefore a first step to anticipating needs and relevant social dialogue. Evaluation of the results regarding the chosen objectives is also an element of a permanent culture of assessment.
Collective Approach	SMEs should not be left alone. They are often at the centre of networks, including other SMEs and larger companies, public institutions in the field of training or employment, professional bodies, federations and social partners. These networks need to be active. In view of the current economic crisis, a collective investment in SMEs will prepare them for the future.

Guidance and Accompaniment	When they step forward, beyond their initial reluctance to receive external guidance offered by professional (chambers of commerce, experience gained by others in their sector, etc.), SMEs can benefit from tailor-made tools to overcome obstacles (financial or organisational) in the field of training. Whether they are within or outside a company (or both), facilitators and enablers correctly trained to do their job can be promoted in their function.
Opportunities	Plenty of opportunities exist for SMEs, but the right information is often missing. SMEs might not always be aware of these opportunities, considering them inaccessible or not intended for them. This is not the case. When correctly equipped and enabled, SMEs can more easily take advantage of these training opportunities, eventually resulting in new economic and social opportunities for the company and its workers.

Source: *Guide for Training in SMEs, European Commission, Directorate-General for Employment, Social Affairs and Equal Opportunities*

2

ANNUAL MAINTENANCE SERVICES: GET COVERED

Having an annual maintenance service plan in place is essential for SMEs, who do not necessarily have extra funds floating around that could finance maintenance or repairs if something were to go irretrievably wrong.

An annual maintenance contract is agreed between an SME and a maintenance provider, and usually consists of a yearly plan which takes measures against all equipment failure and responds to them with their best efforts, should they occur. There are numerous elements to an annual maintenance contract, all of which are just as important as the last.

The regular check and overhaul of equipment is carried out once a year by the maintenance provider. Spare parts are supplied, underlying problems are resolved, follow-up servicing is arranged and the whole system is given an overhaul to identify the parts which aren't doing their job. This is the most important part of the process for many, as it helps to detect problems which are yet to occur and solve them before they cause any damage.

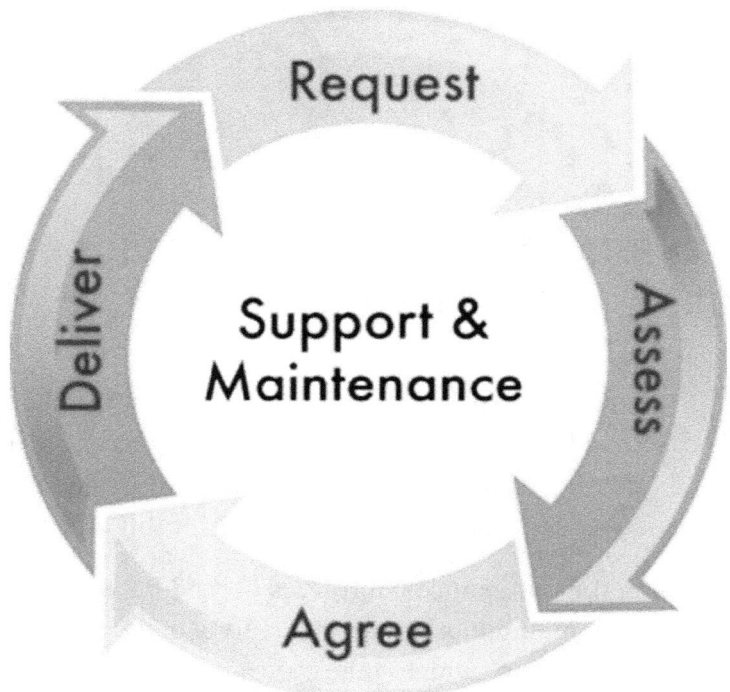

Source: http://www.nashtechsoftware.com/software-development/services/software-support-maintenance-services

The yearly service can also help to troubleshoot and analyse the causes of any issues that might have been found within hardware or software. Based on the analysis, the appropriate action can be taken on the advice of the maintenance professionals.

Parts and technicians can be arranged in a timely manner and the problem will be rectified. This also allows for a regular update on the status of equipment, so that businesses know well in advance when certain things will need to be replaced, when batteries will expire, when new surveys are due, and so on. An entire service history is also provided, so that there is a comprehensive record of any maintenance carried out.

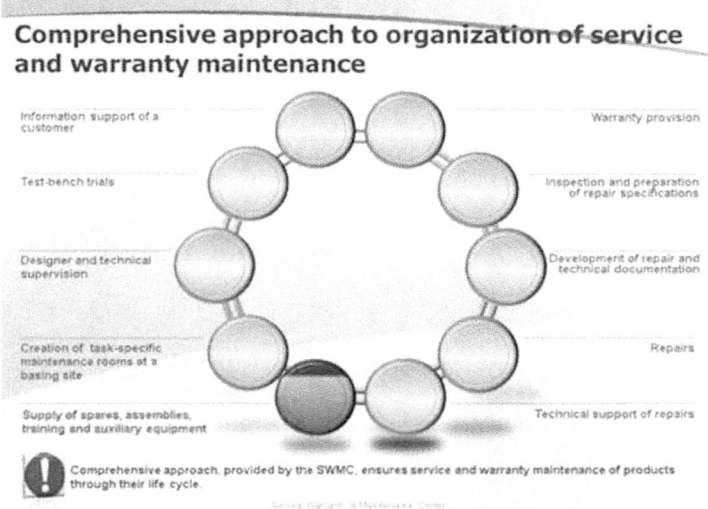

Comprehensive approach to organization of service and warranty maintenance

Source: http://www.avrorasystems.com/eng/m/public/
services/guarantee_maintenance/services.php

There are a multitude of benefits for those who choose annual maintenance plans for their small business. The first is that they can manage their cash flow much more effectively than without a guaranteed maintenance check every year. The sporadic maintenance of hardware and software, or the repair of them when things go wrong due to neglecting to get them serviced, can cost businesses much more than an average annual maintenance contract. The cash flow is more predictable; they know exactly what they are getting from their maintenance provider and they don't need to worry about paying extortionate prices for below par repairs.

3

SOFTWARE ECOSYSTEMS: THE BASICS

Software ecosystems are software solutions which enable, support and automate activities and transactions for the user. They are gaining great prevalence in business across the globe, with popular examples including the Google Android and Apple iOS ecosystems.

The software ecosystem can be defined in accordance with the understanding of the ecosystem in other environments. Human ecosystems are defined as a connection between actors, the activities and transactions between these actors concerning physical or non-physical factors. Commercial ecosystems are systems in which the actors are businesses, customers, partners, suppliers and contractors. The factors are goods and services, and the transactions are financial, with information and knowledge also included.

Ecosystems for software can take various forms, from external developers contributing to the platform of a company, or ecosystems where users contribute knowledge, goods, services and behaviour. Software ecosystems are also commercial ecosystems, providing support for transactions and other business activities which are crucial to everyday operations.

end-user programming	MS Excel, Mathematica, VHDL	Yahoo! Pipes, Microsoft PopFly, Google's mashup editor	none so far
application	MS Office	SalesForce, eBay, Amazon, Ning	none so far
operating system	MS Windows, Linux, Apple OS X	Google AppEngine, Yahoo developer, Coghead, Bungee Labs	Nokia S60, Palm, Android, iPhone
category / platform	desktop	web	mobile

Source: http://www.software-ecosystems.com/Software_ Ecosystems/Definition.html

Companies often have a range of different reasons for implementing a software ecosystem within their operations. Some want to up the value of their current software offering for existing users, some wish to increase the attractiveness of their company to new users, some are focusing more on innovation, and some are collaborating with partners using similar ecosystems.

Converting to a software ecosystem is often the next logical step for a company which has already successfully implemented a platform and intra-organisational software product line. They will generally be built on top of the existing platform, and will extend the functionality of the software which is already in place. Those building the system have complete control over the different software solutions that they can choose, and getting the right mix of programs and applications results in a seamless interface and operation for businesses, which can be expanded on in the future.

Open Source Software Ecosystem

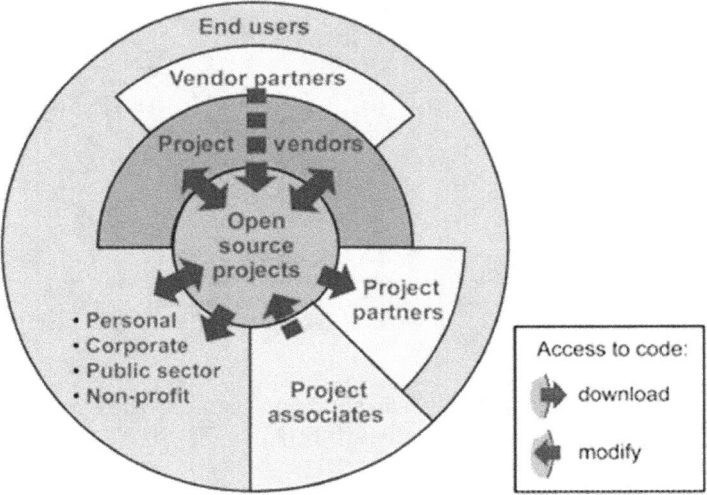

Source: http://www.idc.com/prodserv/maps/opensource.jsp

Return on Investment: Calculate the ROI of your Small Business Software

Return on Investment (ROI) is one of the most popularly used terms in business, and is a phrase which is frequently used to describe the benefits of all business investments.

There are many different criteria by which ROI can be measured, especially for small businesses: has there been a good return on the investments to date? Should investment continue in this vein? Should there be a scaling down or scaling up of the investment? What will be the total investment and the total return over the lifespan of the entire system? In fact, there are a multitude of ways in which ROI can be measured where software is concerned.

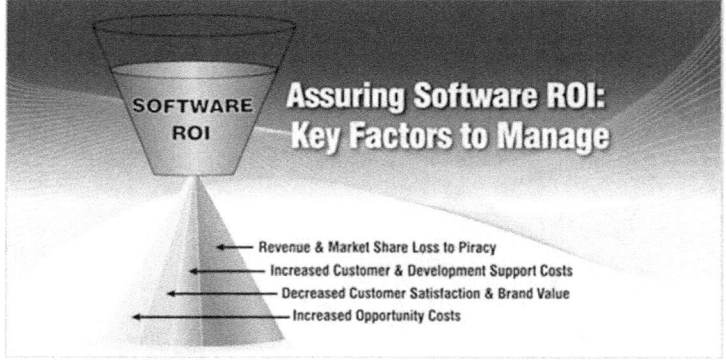

Source: http://www.arxan.com/dont-gamble-with-your-software-roi/

Improved Speed: If a task used to take one day and now takes one hour due to a software upgrade, this is a form of ROI. The more processes which can be carried out in a shorter amount of time, the more money can be made and the more orders can be fulfilled. This is also applicable for customer-facing software; if a search of online products or a database turns up fast results for a customer, they can purchase quickly and boost profits.

Automation: This aspect is in direct relation with improving speed; some organisations get the two confused and try to measure automation when they should be measuring the speed improvements. Automation allows for more informed decisions and can integrate data simply and easily.

Revenue Streams: Business-to-consumer sites can easily measure revenue streams and track their ROI. Improved software for customer-facing elements of a website can directly improve the interface and the usability of revenue streams. If revenue streams are in better condition, it follows that revenue will increase too, boosting ROI.

Communication: The increasing communication that software often offers can be classed as a ROI. It increases the speed at which work can be carried out, and boosts collaboration to create a higher standard of work. Being able to communicate with partners, clients and suppliers in a convenient and efficient way is very important to increasing ROI, as it will facilitate faster working processes and operations.

Compliance: Sometimes policy or legislation dictates that a software update is necessary. In this sense, the return on investment will be adhering to the correct guidelines and not falling foul of company policy. This can be priceless when considering that fines or punishments may come into play for not complying with the rules.

Cost: If a task used to take five servers and one person to carry out, and can now be fully automated, the cost is much reduced. This is perhaps the most obvious way to measure ROI, and the reason that most people invest in certain software upgrades: if costs are reduced, profit margins will increase.

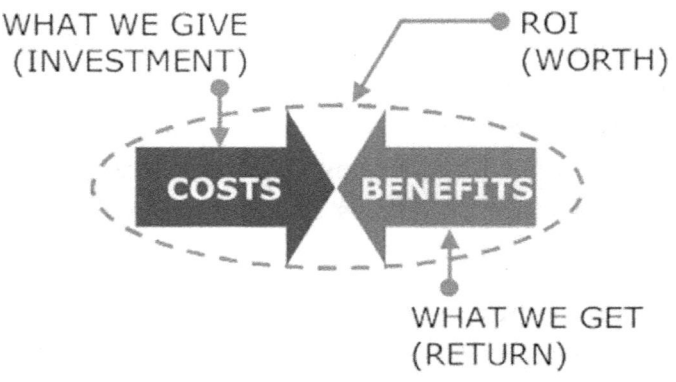

Source: http://blog.mangoapps.com/roi-of-enterprise-social-software/

5

GETTING SUPPORT:
INSOURCING AND OUTSOURCING

Both insourcing and outsourcing are common concepts for businesses around the world, and both have their unique advantages over the other.

They both meet the same demands, but in very different ways, with insourcing typically done within a company's own operational infrastructure, and outsourcing being companies hiring other businesses (which aren't affiliated with the original company) to perform a task or provide a service. Both methods provide cost and resource differences, and they influence a company's management decisions greatly.

Outsourcing is a concept which has seen widespread adoption and implementation by organisations across the globe. Many business owners see outsourcing as a way to cut costs, whilst others prefer to use this method because it frees up crucial time and resources to concentrate on other areas of the business, whether they are marketing or production.

It is important not to mix up outsourcing with offshoring; many in the current market confuse the two, and see the two processes as inseparable, despite the fact that outsourcing work often doesn't leave the originating country.

Insourcing is a more modern concept which has been touted as a viable alternative to outsourcing for many businesses. It is virtually the exact opposite of outsourcing, and involves using in-house staff to fill temporary needs or fulfil certain tasks that would have otherwise been outsourced. This can often mean that the staff members are offered extra training to carry out their new role, which gives them qualifications and a great morale boost.

Rather than sending out the work to external companies, businesses are increasingly choosing to invest in the extensive training of their own staff to ensure they have a core group of individuals who can perform high-specification roles, rather than being under-trained.

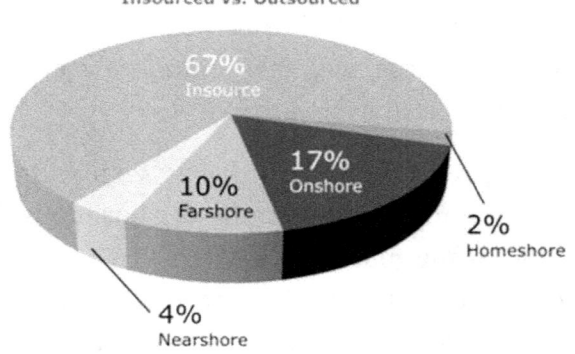

Insourced vs. Outsourced

Source: http://call-center-software.tmcnet.com/topics/call-center-software/articles/57960-outsource-do-it-yourself.htm

Before a business makes a decision about whether they should insource or outsource, it is first recommended that they define their business goals and discuss what they would like to achieve from said insourcing or outsourcing.

Insourcing might seem like a fairly straightforward option, but there are often difficulties in the implementation, such as the time it takes to obtain qualifications and the amount it might cost to train the staff. The long-term effects of insourcing are more beneficial than outsourcing, as they help to create a highly qualified workforce, but those looking for a quick or temporary fix might be better advised to outsource.

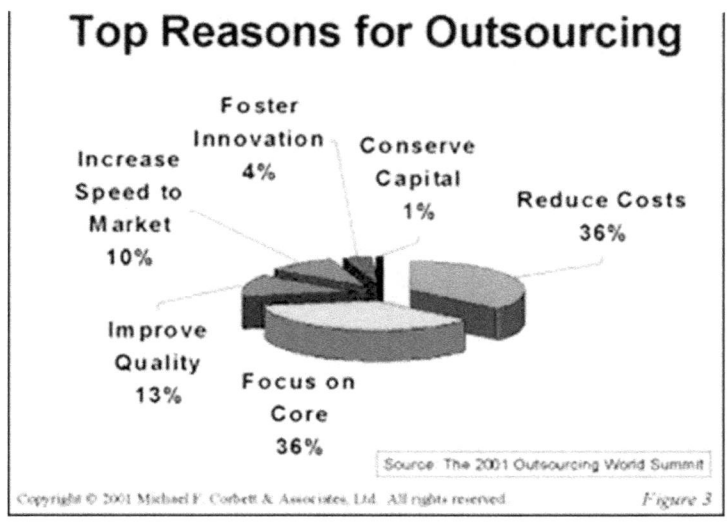

Source: http://eternalsunshineoftheismind.wordpress.com/2013/03/13/outsourcing-whats-so-good-about-it/

If cutting costs is the key objective, outsourcing is the clear winner.

Outsourcing was once considered something of a luxury, something that only larger businesses could invest in, but nowadays companies of all sizes, including start-ups, use outsourcing to free up some of their own time and reduce their outgoings whilst maintaining a level of high-quality service. Outsourcing also offers instant access to experts with specialist skills, rather than waiting for six months or a year for training to be completed.

The drawbacks of outsourcing are that many companies feel uncomfortable with handing some of their most vital processes over to an external provider. It is important to have a high level of trust in the organisation that a task will be outsourced to, and doing a little homework beforehand can go a long way to achieving this.

6

CUSTOMER SUPPORT

No business can survive without its customers. They are the petrol that keeps the engine running. Without them, a business will quickly flounder, which makes customer support a critical concept, particularly for SMEs who often struggle to compete against more established names in the battle to win over hearts and minds.

One of the ways in which SMEs can turn their smaller size to their advantage is in the arena of customer support. The saying that the customer is always right is a little clichéd, but the fact remains that in a competitive marketplace, the customer wields the power and they can afford to be very discerning when it comes to choosing who they do business with.

Investing in systems and taking time to develop processes that improve customer support functions is the key to succeeding. Some customer support processes can be integrated with other business areas. CRM systems are invaluable in this regard and can automate much of the process, from the minute a support ticket needs to be raised to the moment the problem is solved.

A decent CRM system will also help you to identify those customers who are loyal and reward them accordingly, helping to generate goodwill that should safeguard your customer base against snipers. As you start to consider how software and hardware purchases can help to improve customer support, you'll also need to recognise that there is a certain level of innovation needed to make the best of limited resources; and that while technology and applications can solve many problems, they also raise others.

A social media platform, for example, can remove the need to have a dedicated customer service line, as customers can tweet you, or post on a *Facebook* page or even email, rather than call. This frees up resources and on the surface means you are making better use of investments made in those areas. However, it should also be noted that some customers still prefer to use the phone and speak to someone directly and this will need to be addressed when customer support functions are established.

Whether you use the phone in conjunction with social media or simply assign all support functions to your CRM, gathering feedback is essential. You must be able to monitor customer feedback and reviews, in order to be certain your chosen solution is the correct one and able to help resolve customer issues quickly and efficiently.

TECHNOLOGICAL
FRONTIERS

INTRODUCTION

If one thing is certain, it is that technology never stands still. There is always a new tech gold rush, promoted by new companies, new methodologies, new processes, new systems and new ways of doing things. Often, technology frontiers are broken simply by means of finding an even better way to do something, rather than inventing a totally new concept that breaks new ground. Computer memory is one such example. While recent breakthroughs aren't even on the market yet, researchers continue to push through with bigger and more ambitious solutions, such as memory made from glass or crystal and huge new capacities for storing information.

In this chapter we will look at the forerunners in the IT industry, identifying those who are the best in class and pinpointing those who offer best of breed solutions from cradle to grave for small- and medium-sized businesses.

We'll also shed light on future technologies: those breakthroughs that promise to transform the way you do business in 5, 10 or 15 years from now. In the spirit of innovation, we'll also discuss technology lifecycles;

which will determine just how often your business will consider these wonderful, emerging new technologies and how often you can expect to use them for. Finally, to help to put all of that into context, we'll offer the Gartner Analysis, a framework which will help you to recognise confidently the best time to adopt a new technology.

COMING UP

- ◤ Forerunners in IT industry
- ◤ Future Technologies
- ◤ Technology Lifecycle
- ◤ Best time to adopt a new technology: Gartner Analysis

1

FORERUNNERS IN IT INDUSTRY

The IT industry is massively competitive, hugely profitable and littered with companies that make life-changing discoveries and breakthroughs every day. The forerunners in the IT industry make changes that not only improve processes and streamline the way computer systems work, they directly influence how our day-to-day lives unfold and occasionally, become a part of popular culture. What would business be like without Apple's iPhone and iPad tablet? The mobile internet would arguably be in its infancy and the ability to work remotely would also be severely impacted. Even everyday tasks, such as checking email on the move, conference calling while away from the office and using the iPad to surf the net, check competitor websites and presenting the information to clients and suppliers, would all be impossible. Would the landscape of mobile computing be different if BlackBerry hadn't got consumers and business users excited about the prospect of being able to connect to the internet, check calls and even write documents from a handset while on the go? Their stories are ones of innovation and demonstrate the value of doing something truly different, pushing boundaries and reimaging what is possible – all reasons for SMEs to take a leaf out of their playbooks.

The forerunners in the IT industry are the global brands and big names, the household logos that you'll find throughout your home and business. They are brands so familiar that they are literally a part of the furniture – icons that you are so used to seeing that you don't even notice them. But, behind this veil of familiarity, massive things are happening. The likes of Apple and IBM do not rest on their laurels; they constantly strive to find the next big thing, and the next better things. From conquering space to designing totally new materials for computer memory and components, these are the forerunners in the IT industry.

1. Apple. With cutting edge designs and products that break new ground, Apple is responsible for some of the biggest and most mainstream tech innovations in recent years; products such as the iPad, MacBook, notebook, iPhone, iPod, iOS and OSX have a place in offices around the world, helping to make mobile and remote working possible and ensuring managers and workers alike can keep in touch with their offices and colleagues whilst away from their desk at meetings or travelling for business.

2. Samsung. With a sales network, production plants and operations units that span 61 countries and around a quarter of a million staff, Samsung is a powerhouse in the IT industry. It is the largest mobile phone manufacturer and largest television manufacturer in the world, but also the largest computer memory manufacturer and the name behind a series of some of the most exciting computer storage innovations in the world.

3. Hewlett Packard. A famed computer manufacturer, HP also produces a range of technologies, products and software solutions with applications and customers across every major industry.

4. Foxconn. Taiwanese company, Foxconn makes parts for a range of applications including the iPad, iPod and iPhone, making it one to watch in the IT product development stakes.

5. IBM. No other company has had more patents than IBM, which makes it the most pioneering on the planet. From mainframes to servers, hardware to software, it can always be relied upon to push the envelope and re-imagine new ways to carry out IT processes.

2

FUTURE TECHNOLOGIES

A famous law exists known as Moore's Law, which isn't really a law at all, but more an uncannily accurate observation which, for more than half a century, has been used to predict the rate at which future technologies develop.

Named after David E. Moore, who founded Intel, the law is based on a paper that studied computer hardware development historically. In the paper, Moore observed that the number of components in integrated circuits had doubled every year from the invention of the integrated circuit in 1958 until 1965, when the paper was published. A number of computer component developments, including memory capacity and processing speed are linked to this law.

While Moore's Law has been a reliable barometer since the 60s, some believe its effect will be felt less and may be rendered obsolete in the 2020s. For future technologies after that point, we'll have to look elsewhere.

The director of product innovation at SolidWorks, Rick Chin eludes to the fact that the most interesting of future technologies may already be with us. In a list compiled for technology website, Mashable, he says that many existing technologies are very relevant to future visions.

Number one on his list of future technology is the ubiquitous smartphone. Part computer, part phone, a smartphone is a hybrid technology device, whose potential is only just being unveiled. Chin predicts that today's smartphones will become the basis for tomorrow's personal mobile computers (PMC), devices which offer supercomputing speeds from an everyday handset, advanced sensors and personal peripherals, such as glasses, in place of the current screen.

Cloud computing also makes it onto the list of future technologies that will shape the way we live and work. While it is something of a buzzword now, the technology is very much in its infancy and we haven't yet even scratched the surface of what is possible.

Augmented Reality (AR) is already starting to make waves and looks set to be hugely exciting in the near future. Platforms like Blippa have already started to harness AR, with marketing campaigns for the likes of President Obama during his election campaign. In future, this technology could dramatically alter how online marketing is carried out and how we interact with systems. Some brands have already started using AR to let consumers experience virtual products via their web pages, which suggests a lot more is still to come.

Social networking is also predicted to change shape and make use of dynamic and automated network management technology. This will reduce the current burden on the user of managing their connections, and will instead act as a relevance filter, changing the way users interact and connect online.

3

TECHNOLOGY LIFE CYCLE

The TLC or technology life cycle describes the commercial gain made from a product, from its initial concept and development stages, through to it being put to work by the user until it is eventually phased out, upgraded or replaced. In comparison with the life cycle of a product such as concrete, computer hardware, it has a relatively short life cycle; however, it is no less viable, profitable or useful for this relative brevity.

Primarily, the technology life cycle serves to focus on both the time and the cost spent on developing a product. This is then compared with the timeframe needed for costs to be recovered and for the technology to make a profit. The life cycle is not fixed and can be affected by actions outside of its control such as the development of competitor products, which may affect sales, which in turn affects the timeframe needed for the development costs to be offset.

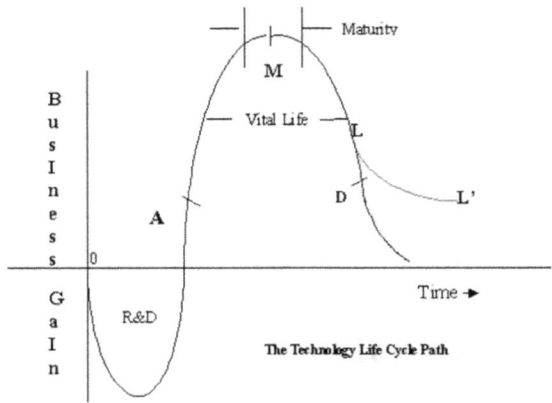

Source: Wikimedia Commons

The technology life cycle is usually split into four distinct stages:

1. Research and Development

2. Ascent

3. Maturity

4. Decline

Best Time to Adopt New Technology

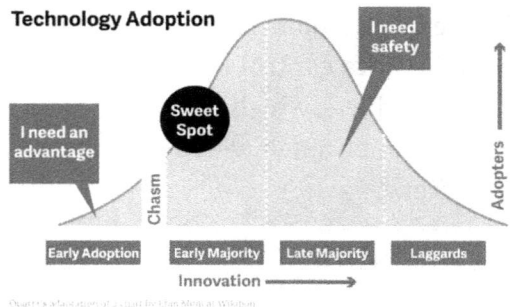

When new technology bursts on to the scene in a flurry of marketing promises and trailblazing excitement, it can be easy to get caught up in the hyperbole and make a rash decision that you may later regret. Adopting new technology can be a very involved, elongated and disruptive process, regardless of the benefits that emerge at the other end.

There are a number of reference methods which determine the speed with which new technologies are adopted and which can act as a framework when wrestling with the difficult question as to when to begin adopting new technology and introducing it into your business environment. One such method is the Technology Adoption Lifecycle Model, which characterises the adoption model according to five groups;

- innovators
- early adopters
- early majority
- late majority
- laggards

An offshoot of this model is the Technology Acceptance Model (TAM) which theorises how users come to accept and then adopt new technology.

"Because new technologies such as personal computers are complex and an element of uncertainty exists in the minds of decision makers with respect to the successful adoption of them, people form attitudes and intentions toward trying to learn to use the new technology prior to initiating efforts directed at using. Attitudes towards usage and intentions to use may be ill-formed or lacking in conviction or else may occur only after preliminary strivings to learn to use the technology evolve. Thus, actual usage may not be a direct or immediate consequence of such attitudes and intentions. (<u>Bagozzi, Davis & Warshaw 1992</u>)"

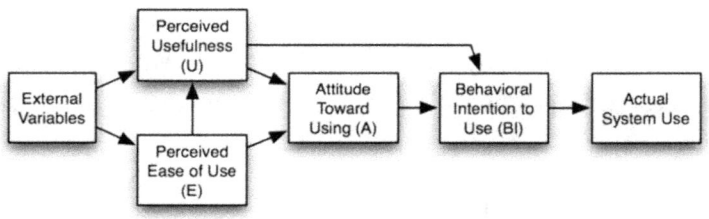

Source: Wikimedia Commons

IT research and advisory firm, Gartner has developed a Hype Cycle which is designed to represent the maturity, adoption and social application of specific technologies. The premise of the Hype Cycle is that it *"...gives you a view of how a technology or application will evolve over time, providing a sound source of insight to manage its deployment within the context of your specific business goals."*

This Hype Cycle can be used as a framework for deciding exactly when new technologies should be adopted. A new cycle is produced each year. The latest one is shown below.

Source: Gartner / Forbes

ABOUT THE AUTHOR

 Vinrose Naluyange is the CEO of Compusoft (U) Ltd, an IT consulting firm. A business woman and author, she was born and raised in Ntinda, a suburb of Kampala city in Uganda. She has acquired a Bsc. information technology at Amity University-India, a diploma in legal studies, and several IT professional certifications. She has more than 9 years' experience advising companies on how to choose the right technology for their businesses.

Vinrose believes that selecting the right technology for any enterprise is one of the critical keys to success. She demonstrates the ways that companies are able to maximize productivity, minimize costs, and get up-to-the minute reports and analyses of employee, customer, and business performance with the proper technology tools in place. These strategies also help companies to stay in contact with their customers, coordinate projects, and integrate work flow in real time. Technology is the next big thing for business. Vinrose's book will guide you in the process of investing in the right technologies to help your business grow and be more profitable.

==

**For more information about Vinrose Naluyange
and Compusoft (U) Ltd, Please go to;
www.compusoftconsult.com**

==